D1321413

THE CHARLES BRIDGE OF PRAGUE

THE CHARLES BRIDGE
OF PRAGUE

KAMIL NOVOTNÝ – EMANUEL POCHE

PHOTOGRAPHED BY JOSEF EHM

PRAGUE PUBLISHING HOUSE V. POLÁČEK, PRAGUE – 1947

I. THE PRAGUE BRIDGE
IN ROMANESQUE TIMES.

The idea of joining the banks of the river at Prague by a bridge was brought into effect right at the dawn of our history, not long after the building of the new seat for the Přemysl dynasty on the Prague castle hill. It arose from the need for a convenient and safe crossing over the river at a time when the castle surroundings or the main seat of the Czech rulers became the centre of the country' and therefore became established as a firm settlement both of native and foreign elements.

As early as the chronicle of Křišťan the news is recorded that St. Wenceslas body at the time of his burial in 932 was brought without hindrance from Stará Boleslav into the St. Guy's church across the bridge, which was at that time partly destroyed by floods. The chronicler Cosmas writes that in the year 1118 the flooded river rose up to 10 ft. above the bridge level. According to that the first Prague bridge was rather low, from which we can deduce that it was only a wooden bridge, for the building technique of stone bridges required until a few centuries later the highly vaulted arches which made the bridge level higher. Besides, as far as we know, there was at that date no other stone erection of such a kind in the whole of Central Europe. Stone bridges, which belonged to the highest technical achievements or ancient times and of the early middle ages, are found then only in areas of Roman building culture, or in places where this had a direct influence, such as Italy, the south of France and Spain. In the rest of Europe stone bridges were erected only towards the end of the Romanesque period, probably with the aid of builders rrom the south of Europe who were experienced in this kind of building.

It seems that the extended research or Romanesque Prague contradicts the supposition that the site of this oldest bridge – or bridges— was indentical with that of the later stone bridge which is the present Charles Bridge. This site was propably for a long time away from the main roads which crossed the ramparts of the castle. Not even the existence of a ford, which is documented by the name or a former church (which has since been destroyed) Sv. Jan na Zábradlí (lat. In vado, i. e. on the ford in the area of the street Na zábradlí) and which was built at the beginning of the 12th century allows the hypothesis that the bridge must have been there from ancient times just because the crossing of the river there was easy. Besides this ford we know that there were two more easy crossings of the Vltava of Romanesque Prague which lie in the axis or the important traffic thoroughfares. There was a ford near the island of Štvanice where the road which led from the area of today's Staroměstské náměstí through Dlouhá and Soukenická třída joined the river bank. There was also a river crossing somewhere in the vicinity of the present Smetanovo náměstí where the road which also started near today's Staroměstské náměstí and led through Kaprova ulice became, on the left bank, twin roads lead-

---

I. The Old Town Bridge Tower. *Peter Parler's* works. 2nd half 14th century.

ing to the Prague castle, one steeply upwards on the Opyš, the second by a detour across the southern ramparts. The more important of the two roads joining the main thoroughfare of Vyšehrad in the area of Staroměstské náměstí is the one which led through Kaprova ulice towards the ducal seat and here we can presume that in all probability there existed the first bridge of Prague.

This original bridge of Prague – whether it was one permanent building or more continuous rebuildings – was destroyed by floods in 1157 or 1159. The time of its destruction is not without significance for the history of a building which was erected here later. It was at the time of the greatest extent of power of the second Czech King, Vladislav, and concurrently at the time of all-embracing and mature building activity in all parts of Romanesque Prague, when in the neighbouring Germany several bridges were being built partly or entirely of stone. If we remember the close political and cultural contact between Bohemia and Germany at that time, if we take into consideration Vladislav's outlook and his considerable ambition, shown amongst many other things in rich building activities, we shall easily understand that the new Prague bridge could not lag behind bridge construction as it then was in Germany. So the new Prague bridge was built this time of stone. It was generally called the Judith Bridge after Vladislav's wife, who took a great interest in the building. The new bridge was not built where its predecessor stood, but more to the south, almost in the same place where the Charles Bridge stands today. The develop-

---

II. Detail of the eastern side of the Old Town Bridge Tower. The seated figures at the bottom are the Emperors Charles IV and Václav IV. *Peter Parler's* works. Circa 1380.

ment of Prague towards the end of the 11th and in the 12th century, and especially of the quarter on the left bank of the river Vltava where several new churches were built, and also the new situation of traffic on the right bank, created by the movement and growth of settlements and new buildings, demanded new main traffic routes between the two banks of Prague and also a bridge of rather different character. The new bridge had not to serve merely as a link between the people's living quarters on the right bank of the Vltava and the royal seat on Hradčany, but as a convenient and fuller connection between the two parts of the castle's surroundings. For this bigger purpose the ford across the river near the church of St. John na Zábradlí, which has already been mentioned, seemed more convenient than the site of the former bridge, and therefore the new bridge was founded here, further to the south than its predecessor. One of the followers of Cosmas, the chronicler Vincencz, writes about the building, which was one of the most important technical undertakings erected in Prague up to that time, and remarks that Queen Judith built the bridge within three years. He does not say however which three years. This statement is, from what we know about the slow building tempo of the middle ages, the less credible as it concerns a building which was without precedent in Bohemia and which was technically very difficult. Therefore even the older historians of the bridge tried to explain Vincenc's incredible report by suggesting that the building was probably only partly built of stone – that it had only

---

III. Old Town Bridge Tower. Western side. 2nd half 14th century. First floor repaired 1649–50.

stone pillars – whereas the rest was wooden. This is however not borne out by a report from 1348 which, speaking about the Judith Bridge, says expressly that it was a stone bridge, and the newer archaeological findings and the study of the remains of the building confirm the statement from 1348. It seems that Vincenc's statement concerns only the final phase of the building, although the whole building process had been going an for same years before. As we have no reliable historical reports we can assume the approximate beginning and end of the building from our knowledge of the dates of King Vladislav. The most likely time of the beginning of this building is given by three data: the not quite accurately known date of the destruction of the old wooden bridge already mentioned i. e. 1157 or 1159 and the year 1158 when Vladislav returned from the famous expedition to Milan loaded with loot which gave him the opportunity to begin such a costly enterprise, and also the year 1159 when Vladislav gave same estates near the bridge for the building of a church and a Maltese monastery. The terminus ante quem of the foundation of the bridge is then the year 1172 when Vladislav gave up the throne. It follows that the bridge could have been begun and probably also finished only during these fourteen years.

Another problem of the history of this second Prague bridge building is the question of the builder. It is certain that the builder could scarcely have been a local man for there was no experience in such constructions. Only a foreigner well versed in the calculations

IV. Southern side of the bridge with the Island of Kampa. The statue on the pillar in the foreground is Šimek's statue of Bruncvik from 1884.

of construction and in the intricate art of making the bridge pillars, only a man who knew how they are walled and who knew especially the technique and the complicated execution of the arching of the vaults of the bridge could have been the builder. Such bridges were a rarity even in Germany at that time and the only perfect and nearest bridge which could possibly have been the model was the stone bridge of Regensburg, built probably between 1135 – 1146. The bridge of Regensburg is, in the particularities of its construction and the manner of building, so near to the bridge of Prague that the connection is without any doubt. Also certain historical facts speak for it: the old cultural connection between Regensburg and Prague, and indeed the connection between the whole area of Bavaria and Bohemia in romanesque times, of which we have many confirmations in the close relationship of buildings in both countries. And above all there is the fact that King Vladislav knew the bridge of Regensburg – probably the most perfect work of its kind in Germany – from his own experience, as he was crowned in Regensburg in 1158. We can therefore easily assume that when, at the end of the fifties of the 12th century, he was faced with the necessity of the reconstruction of the bridge in his own capital, he called upon the builder whose work he had seen shortly before at his coronation in Regensburg.

But yet this building enterprise was scarcely directed by a German artist or technician. The conditions of bridge building in romanesque Germany does not indicate that this was a German home trade,

---

1. St. Ivo. *František Hergesel's* copy from 1908 of the original group of *Matyáš Braun's* from 1711. Sandstone.

but that in this the Germans were dependent on the help and experience of south European builders, especially those from northern Italy, where bridge building was, from ancient times, on a high level of perfection, and where there could be found examples closely resembling the Regensburg bridge. If we then remember the power of the influence of Italian architecture in the form and decoration of Bavarian buildings in the 10th – 12th centuries, and especially in the architecture of Regensburg, we may assume that the builder of the Regensburg bridge, a work which was exceptional for its time – came from southern Europe, most probably from northern Italy. The connection between the bridges in Regensburg and Prague leads then to the logical conclusion that the Judith Bridge was the work of an Italian, or better, the work of hands which were directed by the knowledge and experience of an Italian artist.

Only small parts remain of the Judith Bridge to give us an idea of its situation and form. This situation was not quite the same as that of today's Charles Bridge, but was rather more to the north-east. We can see where the two ends were from the towers, which have been more or less preserved for us, and which evidently defended the crossing since the building of the bridge under Václav I in the 13th century. The tower on the right bank is hidden in the walls of the salient which juts out from the south-west end of the main block of the Convent of the Cross. This adaptation was effected during the rebuilding of the convent by Carlo Lurago in the third quarter of the 17th century. The followers of the chronicler

2. *Matěj Václav Jäkl*. The Madona with St. Bernard. 1709. Sandstone.

Cosmas mention the tower for the first time in the year 1251. It had an entrance gate on the ground level and was built on the first pillar of the bridge. This pillar, as well as the opposite one and the arch between them, could be seen until the forties of the last century, when the area was covered by the levelling of the ground for the erection of the Charles IV statue. The opposite end of the Judith Bridge, on Malá Strana, was in the same place as that of Charles Bridge. This can be seen quite plainly from the southern smaller tower on the left bank, which was probably built at the same time as the bridge and the opposite bridge tower on the right bank, during the fortification of the old city. The tower on the Malá Strana side is first mentioned in 1249, when, during the rebellion of Přemysl II against his father Václav, the tower fell into the hands of the young prince. It was repaired and again fortified by Václav I, which proves that it had been in existence for some time. It was probably built to defend the approach to the bridge from the area of Malá Strana, which was then not yet fortified, and so it added to the fortified strength of the bridge on the opposite side. Unlike the tower on the eastern, the Old Town end of the bridge, the traffic did not pass through the main body of the tower, but as today, through a gate which was inset between the two towers. This gate and the northern tower did not, however, remain in their original state, but were replaced in the course of the 15th century by new buildings in the later Gothic style. Several archaeological and historical facts bear witness that before the

---

3. *Ferdinand Max Brokoff*. Ss. B a r b a r a, M a r g a r e t and E l i s a b e t h. 1707. Sandstone.

erection of the gate and its Gothic tower there was here another older gate and tower in either late romanesque or early Gothic style, which meant that there existed a free entrance to the bridge between the two towers. The main fact is that on the ground floor of the existing southern tower there is no trace of any gate onto the bridge, from which it follows that the traffic on the bridge led outside the tower. Its exact route can be seen from the remains or pillars and arches of the Judith Bridge found in the cellar of the house No. 78-III, and under the no longer existing house No. 84-III at the corner of Lužická street. If we connect these remains by an imaginary axis which we then extend towards the bridge tower on the Malá Strana we shall find that the bridge led here to the north of the tower, to the area of today's Gothic gate. As the bridge became a part of the fortifications, after the fortification system of the Old Town of Prague and of the lesser town of Prague was completed in the second and third quarters of the 13th century, it is very unlikely that the traffic led across the bridge after the erection of the ramparts, and the gates of the town would have been free on this side, and would not have been secured by a tower as well as by a gate which could always be closed. If then the gate was built on to the northern side of the tower, there follows, according to the mediaeval system of fortification, the existence of a second tower which stood on the other, the northern, side of the gate. The existence of this tower can be deduced from historical sources. We learn from a deed of 1409 (in the Archives of the City of

---

4. *Matěj Václav Jäkl.* The Madona with Ss. Dominic and Thomas Acquinas. 1708. Sandstone.

Prague No. 993) which contains a notification of an exchange of a house called the Saxon No. 55-III, next to the lesser bridge tower and which belonged to Rudolf III the Duke of Saxony, for a house called the Naza on Perštýn, that, together with the house, the townsmen of the Old Town received both towers on the sides of the gate (i. e. the gate leading to the bridge). These towers and the gate were however not the same as the buildings which stand there today, for the present bridge tower – as judged by the heraldic ornamentation showing the might of the Czech King as it was towards the end of the reign of Václav IV in 1411 – could have originated only after this year. The present higher bridge tower on the Malá Strana side was built in the second quarter of the 15th century before 1451. It follows that the gate of the bridge and one of the two towers mentioned in the deed of 1409 and which, according to what we have already said, must have been the northern tower, cannot be the same as the present northern tower and the gate, and that before the erection of these parts of the present fortifications on the bridge on the Malá Strana side there was here a similar configuration which was no doubt the remains of the old bridge of Judith. This is borne out indirectly by other historical reports. The property of the Dukes of Saxony on Malá Strana together with everything that belonged to it – i. e. including the bridge fortification – came to the Saxon family in 1348, before the foundation of the Charles Bridge. Between this year and the year 1409, from when we have the report about both bridge

---

I. The picture of the bridge of *E. Sadeler*, shown opposite, from 1606, is one of the oldest and most exact, and shows the bridge in its original Gothic form. The bridge's silhouettes strictly horizontal. The many statues of calvary and stages of the cross form a plastic stafage. On the tower can be seen the outlines of Gothic sculptury, which was destroyed in 1648.

M

I. K

towers and gate, there is no mention anywhere of such buildings being built here, and it is also highly improbable that a private owner such as the Duke of Saxony would build a public fortification to the bridge on his own ground. Both the towers and the gate, which existed at the time that the Duke left his property, were evidently standing before he entered into it, that is, before 1348. There is a remark in the report of the chronicler František Pražský of 1301 which mentions the rebuilding of the Bishop's estate on the Malá Strana which was situated to the northwest of the bridge. He says that Bishop Jan IV from Dražice built a granary as far as the bridge tower. He could not have built this granary up to the southern tower, because he would then have been building across the traffic lane to the bridge, and therefore the tower mentioned by František Pražský could only have been the tower on the northhern side of the bridge which bordered immediately onto the Bishop's estate. From all these sources it can be deduced almost with certainty that the present lesser tower on Malá Strana, the only remnant of the ancient Judith Bridge, was not an isolated building but was probably part of a group of two towers and a gate which were a unit both in building and in style, and has stood in its changed form from the first half of the fifteenth century up to the present day.

The form of the bridge can be relatively easily reconstructed from its remains. Apart from the pillars and arches on both banks which have been already mentioned, there is a series of the foundations of the pillars in the eastern half of the river (at low water in 1784 twelve were noticed, and in 1940 41 some were also seen). They lie towards the south-western salient of the Convent of the Cross, which masks the former bridge tower. According to these remnants the bridge was 6.8 metres wide and 513.90 metres long. The diameter of the arches of the bridge was 10.94 metres and they rested on mighty pillars of unequal thickness – between 7–11 metres – built of red sandstone with inserted blocks of opuka stone. These pillars in turn rested on pilots with a kind of lying grill and were bolstered against the current with three - sided capitols. The vaulting arches consisted of rhomboids of finely hewn rough sandstone. There was a 1 metre high, 0.35 metre wide stone balustrade on the bridge, which was paved with irregular pieces of quartz cemented together with mortar. There were runnels to let out the rain water; in fact the whole bridge was not very dissimilar, either in the manner of building or in the system of fortification, from the present Charles Bridge. The main difference lay in the height, for the pavement of the Judith Bridge was 4–5 metres lower than the pavement of the present bridge, and in the number of pillars, of which there were more. There were approximately six pillars of the Judith Bridge to every five of the Charles Bridge, so that the range of pillars was thicker, and the arches smaller.

There was one more similarity between the two bridges, past and present, and that is the statue ornamentation on the front of the lesser bridge tower of Malá Strana, which seems to be the forerunner of the later plastics which enrich the wall of the tower at the Old Town end of Charles Bridge. This is a relief made of opuka stone placed in the niche of what is today the first floor of the eastern side of the tower, and which shows a religious figural scene of unknown meaning. On the left of a seated figure facing forwards – no doubt representing the Emperor – of which only the body is left, we see the kneeling figure of a bare-headed young man in a tunic. (The head is at present in the Museum of the City of Prague.) This relief, which could formerly be seen from

5. *Emanuel Max*. P i e t y (View with the cross) 1859. Sandstone.

the bridge, was covered in the 16ᵗʰ century by the building of a small house No. 56-III, and later, in the last century, was completely blocked by the building of a wooden cabin. It was rediscovered in 1888, later built over again, and was refound only in 1938 when it was conserved by the care of the Club for Ancient Prague. The group, which was originally brightly coloured, and which belongs to the period of later romanesque sculpture, originated towards the end of the first half of the 13ᵗʰ century. If we believe the supposition of Merhout, that this sculpture represents the historical event of the subjugation of Přemysl II to his father Václav I after the miscarried rebellion in 1249, and as we know from the report of a follower of Cosmas that there were erected 1254, after Václav's death, as he says "in foro" (in the open), stone pictures to commemorate the dead king, then we need not exclude the possibility that the relief is one of these memorials, erected in this important thoroughfare partly because the tower played an important part in Přemysl's rebellion. The relief is a work of very high standard which by far surpasses the Czech plastic art of that time, and it is therefore probable that it is the work of a foreign artist who was well versed in the means of contemporary French sculpture.

There is a supposition that, besides the relief, the Judith Bridge was also decorated by a head of the so-called Bearded Man, which was formerly placed on an arch of the bridge under the Convent of the Cross, and which was transferred in the middle of the

---

5a. *Jan Brokoff.* Piety with the angels. Copper engraving of Augustine Neuräutter's from the drawing by Karel Kulík of 1714. This group, built on the bridge in 1695, is today in the garden of the Monastery of Sisters of Mercy in Prague III.

*Prænobili Generoso ac Consultiss.mo Viro, Domino Bohuslao Joanni Woržikowský de
Kundratiz Primati Regiæ Urbis Capitalis Vetero-Pragenæ meritissimo, ef super Legionis Cívico-Militár em
supremo Aquilæ Præfecto observantissimo, nec ñ ac Regiam fiscarum Deputationem ex partestatuum Cissceri hono
randissimo, Æcænigiotus vere nacto et Boleroso ejusd in Matris Cultori perquam singulari Patrone suo semper Co
lendissimo, hanc in Celeberrimo Pontis Pragenæ sub Primatu ejus ab Augustissimo prædicta Vetis-Magistratu Magnificam
Artis struen Publico cultui positam hic vero colebo incisam*

D.D.D.

*Augustin, Neuraitter civis
ibidem servi obseqmo*

last century to the embankment wall next to the Charles Bridge. The present state of this plastic makes it hard to decide whether it was really an original part of the bridge, or whether it is a work of later origin brought here from elsewhere. The oldest report about the Bearded Man dates from the flood year of 1432, when the head was used to measure the high water.

The Judith Bridge lasted only two centuries. It stood up to partial destruction in 1272, but could not withstand the force of ice logs and other material which the floods of the 3rd February 1342 carried down. It was torn and destroyed in several places so that only one third remained, and it was therefore for a long time of no practical use. This decided its fate. The catastrophe to this building, which was considered as one of the wonders and the pride of Prague, was counted by contemporaries to be a national misfortune. The chronicler František Pražský, writing about its destruction, describes the catastrophe in desperate pathetic words. "As if the crown of the kingdom had fallen when that famous bridge came down" he writes in his lament.

6. Calvary. The bronze corpus of Christ from the period before 1657, sandstone pedestal with an inscription from 1707, the statues of the Madonna and St. John Evangelist are of sandstone and were carved by *Emanuel Max* in 1861.

II. THE CHARLES BRIDGE.

A city as highly developed as the Prague of the end of the reign of John of Luxemburg could not, of course, be without a permanent connection between the two river banks, and therefore after the catastrophe to the Judith Bridge, it was replaced by a new wooden bridge. It is not known exactly where it stood, but it certainly could not have been far from the site of its predecessor because of the existing traffic lanes. The original intention was to rebuild the broken bridge from the proceeds of its own excise, especially from the customs and bridge toll which had been collected since 1252 for the maintenance of the bridge by the monks of the Order of the Cross, and from the custom collected according to the toll order since 1348 on the wooden provisional bridge. This custom was originally meant for the rebuilding of the

---

7. *Josef Max.* St. Joseph. 1854. Sandstone.

stone bridge, but the idea of the mere rebuilding of the bridge, which was mentioned at the beginning of the reign of Charles IV, disappeared in the fifties of that century. The Emperor who made Prague the first city of Central Europe and of the whole empire by the foundation of the University, of innumerable churches and convents, and even by the foundation of a completely new quarter called the New City of Prague, felt that here too nothing must be spared, and that a new bridge must be built, firmer and broader than the old, which should meet the increased requirements of the times and of the blossoming city. As soon as the means were secured, partly from the excise of the old bridge and to a greater extent from the church collections made throughout the kingdom, the foundation stone of the new bridge was laid, later than had been intended, on the 9th July 1357. The building was entrusted to a young builder, Peter Parler, then only twenty-seven years old, who had been called to Prague not long before from Swabian Gmuend, to continue the building of the St. Guy Cathedral after Mathias of Arras. The Old Town foundation of the bridge was laid near the former Convent of St. Kliment, so that the new bridge went rather southwards as compared with the old. This was enforced by changes in the local conditions. The importance of Staroměstské náměstí (the Old Town Square), of the Týn Church, and of a new traffic lane going towards Prašná Brána (the Powder Tower) necessitated a shorter and more direct connection with the bridge. This led through the present Karlova ulice (Charles Street)

7a. *Jan Brokoff.* St. Joseph. Neuräuter's copper engraving from the drawing by Karel Kulík from 1714. This statue, built on the bridge in 1706, is today in the country lapidarium.

ITE
AD
IOSEPH

Illustrissimæ Dominæ D. Teresiæ Drzichowskiana, natæ e Comitibus de Wer-
schowetz, Hanc S. Josephi Bohemiæ Patroni, Nutritij et fidelis servi
Iesu, Statuam lapideam in Ponte Pragensi suis sumptibus erectam;
nunc vero eclsho incisam dat, consecrat
Augustin Neurautter

C. Robel del.   8   A. Neurautter sculp.

and it superceded the former way through Platnéřská ulice. The expenses of the bridge were borne not only by the Emperor himself, but also by the clergy and later by the whole population; collections of fines for indulgences were made in churches, the fines ordered by the church tribunals were sent for the building of the bridge, and the builders also received some bequests. The expense of the building, and also some serious technical obstructions, particularly in the founding of the pillars, caused the building time to be unexpectedly prolonged. We know that in 1367 (ten years after the laying of the foundation stone) the provisional wooden bridge was still in use, and that that year the bridge was again broken up by floods which also broke one pillars of the new bridge. The first reliable information on the completion of the Charles Bridge – as it was called only after 1870 – appears in 1406, when we hear of a small toll house for collecting toll and excise from pedestrians and horsemen on "the new stone bridge". This description "the new stone bridge" is repeated again in 1432, when there is mention of the Charles Bridge being damaged by floods. It was then broken down in three places. This does not mean of course that the building of the bridge road was drawn out so long into the fifteenth century. The new bridge was already in use in the eighties of the fourteenth century, for in 1383 Václav IV ordered an excise on everything brought across the bridge to the Malá Strana. But the work on the bridge went on even in the fifteenth century. The bridge-builders – fabrica pontis – are still

---

8. *Matěj Václav Jäkl.* St. Anne (Mother of the Virgin Mary). 1707. Sandstone.

working full strength, if not on the bridge itself, repairing the damage caused by frequent floods, then on the towers, and for this reason the date of the final completion of the bridge escapes the attention of the chroniclers and the bridge was called new at a time when it had long since been in use. It was chiefly the foundation of the bridge towers and the expensive work on them that retarded the completion of the building. The Judith Bridge was taken as an example for the fortification of the new bridge, which, like the old, was secured on the Old Town bank by one, on the Malá Strana bank by two towers. On the Old Town end of the bridge the urban situation had changed, whereas the disposition of the town fortifications on the left bank remained as they were, probably owing to the then century old fortifications of the Malá Strana and the well-balanced groundplan of the bridge's surroundings. This different disposition of the bridge towers, which was a heritage from the former Judith Bridge, and which does not correspond with the direction of the new bridge, accents the fact that the axis of the new bridge does not enter the gate of the Malá Strana straight, but at a blunt angle.

The bridge tower on the Old Town side, which follows stylistically the example of the older tower form, was founded by Peter Parler at about the same time as the bridge, but the building of it was prolonged at least until the beginning of the 15th century. Apparently it was finished up to the first storey before the death of Charles IV. This part of the tower probably originated in the

9. St. Francis Xaverius. *Čeněk Vosmík's* copy of 1911 of *Ferdinand Max Brokoff's* original group of 1711. Sandstone.

last five years of his reign, for above the gate there are the coats of arms of countries which under Václav IV, Charles successor, did not all belong to the Czech crown. The coat of arms of Lower Lusatia, which was won for the Czech crown in 1373, is especially telling for the date of the foundation of the tower, and also the coat of arms of the town of Zhořelec, which, together with part of Lower Lusatia, was lost to the crown in 1377. Therefore we may assume that this part of the tower was erected in 1377 at the latest. The upper storeys were built in the last quarter of the 14th century. The kingfisher motive, an emblem which appears on artistic works only during the time of Václav IV, and the placing of a statue of Václav next to that of his father on the first storey of the tower, prove that this part was built after Charles' death. The appearance of Václav as a grown-up bearded man (he was born in 1361) fixes the date of its erection in the last but one decade of that century. The tower was finished at the beginning of the next century. On the left bank one of the towers of the old Judith Bridge was used. It is today the lesser Malá Strana tower, which was at one time partially destroyed and devastated during the frequent skirmished, mainly at the beginning of the 14th century when this side of the bridge and of the town fortifications was an important strong point. Next to the bridge tower, which was built some time after 1411, there was erected only one higher tower of Malá Strana, and this was completed only in the reign of Jiří (George) of Poděbrady in 1451. It is not known when the founda-

---

II. *Ouden-Allen's* view of the bridge about 1685 illustrates its appearance shortly before the baroque sculptural redecoration. The calvaries are replaced by new baroque works, the stages of the cross have already disappeared. The western side of the tower has been rebuilt, and is as it appears today.

tions were laid, but certainly not until after 1420. The style, even of the lower floors, shows that it was built in the second quarter of the 15th century, and this fact is indirectly borne out by reports from other sources, particularly a mention in a chronicle of Vavřinec of Březová and also in the chronicle of the University of Prague where, in describing a fight between the citizens of Prague and Sigmund's army in 1420, mention is made of only one bridge tower on Malá Strana, which can only be the present lesser tower.

The Charles Bridge is the fourth bridge of our country. Although it came after the Judith Bridge and the bridges of Písek and Roudnice, its building technique is not different from that of its predecessors. We see the repetition of the set contemporary style, though it is of course more thorough, as befits the importance of the building, the builder and the spaciousness ($515 \cdot 76 \, m \times 9 \cdot 40 \, m$). In appearance then it does not widely differ from the contemporary or older buildings of its kind in our country or abroad. The pillars rest in the same fashion on a socalled grill, they are of exactly equal strength (the width varying between $8 \cdot 50$–$10 \cdot 84$ metres) in order to balance the shallow foundation by the weight of the mass, they have the same three-sided capitols and are connected by the same half-circled, broadly extended arches, of which there are sixteen. The bridge of the town of Roudnice, then recently built, probably served as a model. It was certainly a convenient fact that the builder of the Roudnice bridge, William of Avignon, had schooled local builders who, either themselves or through their pupils, took part in the building of the Charles Bridge. The inscription in the St. Guy Cathedral names Peter Parler as the builder of the Charles Bridge, but probably in fact he was merely the man who "directed the bridge across the Vltava" as the inscription says, for owing to his lack of the necessary experience he had to used experienced and expert helpers. And here we should look in vain for traces of his activities, for only on the Old Town bridge tower do we find pronounced examples of Parler s art, especially on the facade which looks towards the Old Town itself. There are not only architectoincal motives which are typical of Parler's building, such as the unbroken arch and the character of the application of the statues, but also the whole spirit of the building, which shows that it was carried out according to a unified plan without later changes, even though the building was completed only after the planner's death in 1399. This is borne out by the conception, which follows one and the same thought firmly in both directions – the height of both storeys is the same and at the same time their height is a repetition of the proportions on the ground floor, given by the distance of the cornice of the first storey from the consoles which begin the arch of the gateway and the corner pinnacle; the number of the parts is doubled horizontally with their ascent towards the main cornice, so that the halves into which the bottom of the tower is divided by the croos flower of its gate arch correspond with the four parts of the first storey, and to them again the eight panelled parts of the second storey.

Also in accordance with the unity of the architectonical display is the rounded fashioning and the formal relationship of the plastic decoration, which is in this respect, as well as in its subject matter, really a speciality of its period. To some extent there is a repetition of the idea of the plastic decoration of the triforium of the St. Guy Cathedral, such as in the accumulation of the realistic portrait figures next to the idealised statues of the saints, witnessing the great self-confidence of the builders of the tower, who did not hesitate to put up their own monument beside

---

10. *Karel Dvořák*, St. Cyril and Method. 1938. Sandstone.

that to the Czech patron saints. And what is more, they did not put their own figures with the pretence of being religious and humble donators, but as independent enthroned figures, full of the dignity of the individual freed from the humiliating serfdom of the mediaeval ideas of the life beyond the grave and of the fate after death. As a prophesy of the future renaissance of the faith in man and his physical and mental values, there are enthroned in the first storey of the eastern front of the tower the stone figures of Charles IV and Václav IV. Between them is the figure of St. Guy, the patron of the bridge, and above them, on the second storey, are the standing figures of St. Adalbert and St. Sigismund. The sculptury on the second side of the tower, facing the bridge, showing the enthroned Madonna in the traditional conception and the kneeling Charles IV with one of his queens, was alas destroyed during the battles on the bridge in 1648, and it is known only from a primitive illustration of the older Prague vedutists. All the plastic work on the tower which has been preserved, the figures described above and also the smaller figural consoles beneath the corner pinnacles, are, like the whole of the architecture, the collective work of Parler's St. Guy building undertaking. The whole creation, though not homogeneous in its formal nuances or in technique, is yet stylistically one, and was all in the process of building during the last twenty years of the 14th century.

The whole of the tower is a well-solved combination of usefulness and decorativeness, both functions of the tower, as it had

10a. *Ferdinand Max Brokoff*. St. Ignacius of Loyola. Copperplate of Neuräutter's from a drawing by Karel Kulík from 1714. This group, built on the bridge in 1711, is today in the country lapidarium.

Admodum Reverendo, Religiosissimo, et Clarissimo Patri in Christo Patri Francisco Wölcker,
e Societate Jesu SS. Theologiæ Doctori, in Alma Cæsareo-Regia, Universitate Carolo Ferdinandeą Pragensi
ejusdem SS. Theologiæ Regio Professori Emerito, nec non Libris censendis Societatis Regiæ ad S. Clementem
Rectori dignissimo, hanc, in Latium conversionem, Magistri operosi, curâ studioq; adlaborata, in
Celeberrimo Regio Pragensi, ad Matrem Hospitalium mestè sunt coluptum; sui luminis ergà in-
clytum Neo-Pragense Ignatianum Collegium, observantiæ Symbolum, D. D.

Jub AdmirÆdiu et Cleneus Gubernatis.

obsequiens Cliens

Aug. Neuraüther Civis R. auchographi, Vet: Prag: X.

not only to defend the entrance to the bridge, but also to be an artistically impressive entrance, worthy of such a great masterpiece. Birnbaum wrote of the tower: "It was indeed in all probability the most beautiful tower in Europe at that time, remarkable not only for its refined richness, but also for the fact that it ingeniously includes in the decoration the facts given by the construction and purpose of the tower; the shield motive, which dominates the decoration of the first storey is a kind of artistic replica of the apertures in the gate, just as the panelling of the second storey is a development of the horizontal which is given by the main cornice and the battlements. The whole work gains thereby an effect of the utmost individuality and originality, completely free from schematisicism." Thexduty of the tower as part of the fortifications is shown by its situation, its massive walls, the placing of its decorations on the surface of its bulk, and by the small corner towers, aptly called "sentinals" by the French (échauguettes). Owing, however, to the rich figural ornamentation on the main facade surfaces, and to the placing of the tower in the axis of the bridge, the main purpose is almost obscured and the heavi ness of the tower becomes lightened. This is also helped by the applied ornamentation which is enlivened with busts like those of the St. Guy's triforium. These statues are perhaps rather less realistic in gesture and in the conception of a different and unusual treatment of the whole figure, but theyn evertheless show the same tendency towards realism.

---

11. *Emanuel Max,* St. Christopher. 1857. Sandstone.

The model of the Old Town tower was one which was often repeated in our country. We should remember Viollet le Duc's "la ville des échauguettes", as he called Prague, to realise the whole genealogy which begins with the bridge and reaches its height in the Powder Tower. This also explains the great similarity of the larger Malá Strana tower to the Old Town (Staroměstské) tower, the analogy of its construction and the identity of its form. The two towers differ however in their articulation and details of decoration, which date from a time when values in building had begun to change. The later Gothic style of the second quarter of the 15th century appears in the Malá Strana tower in the broken rectangular form of the walls, the expansion of the applied ornamentation and the freedom of the jointing, which is far away from the mathematically exact relationship between the individual parts of the Old Town tower. The tower is here divided into three storeys by slightly projecting cordons, but, unlike the vertical division of the Old Town tower, the two bottom storeys are low in relation to the top one, which, by its disproportionate height helps to create an impression of the loftiness of the whole building. This is also emphasized by the slenderness of the roof and accepted in the measurements of the small corner towers and of the pinnacles over the niches on the front surface. The decoration is considerably restricted, certainly in order to reduce the cost, but this in no way deducts from the effect of the tower. The plainer surface is counterbalanced by a firmer cohesion of the individual

12. *Josef Max*, St. John the Baptist. 1855. Sandstone.

parts, which is particularly evident in the organic inclusion of the small corner towers.

The bridge was finally completed almost a hundred years after the laying of the foundations. But this does not mean that its definite structure was then completed. The tooth of time, the destructive force of the water, the ruins of wars as well as the new practical and aesthetical requirements caused – even up to the present day – alterations to the building and its decoration. When it was scarcely finished the bridge was destroyed in three places by floods in 1432, so that a large part of the money intended for its perfection had to be devoted to repairs. The task of caring for the building was entrusted by Václav I to the monks of the Order of the Cross in the middle of the 13th century. In 1342 however, the district of the Old Town of Prague took it over, and it has derived economic as well as juridical benefit from it for centuries. For this purpose an "office of the Prague bridge" was set up, though it is not known when, possibly even during the reign of Charles IV. This office was endowed with the river banks of Malá Strana and Smíchov, and was directed since 1448 by four town officials and a scribe, who kept the accounts of the bridge office. The oldest reports of this office are from the year 1436, the time when the Old Town officials took possession of the hospital of the Order of the Cross and all the rights and duties concerning the bridge. The revenue from the bridge came from different sources. There was firstly the tolls and excise which were

12a. *Jan Brokoff*, The Lord's Christening. Copperplate of Neuräutter's from a drawing by Karel Kulík from 1714. This group, built on the bridge in 1706, is today in the country lapidarium.

A: M: D: G:
Et Ignatij Raphaelis Honori
Ioannes Fridericus Neuman
à Neüberg
Vet: Pragæ Vir Consularis, Ca=
ritatis, Equestris, et officij
Ions Pontis, Inspector
fieri fecit

Aᵒ: 1706

Prænobili, Generoso et Consultissimo Viro, Domino Ioanni Friderico Neuman
Nobili de Neüberg, Regiæ Urbis Veteris Pragensis senatori meritissimo, equiti, Civico Vetero=
Pragensium Magistro strenuo et officij Pontis Pragensis Inspectori Vigilantissimo SSᵐæ Trinitatis et sancti
Ioannis Baptistæ zelatori serventissimo, ejusceq̃ in lapide excusæ Pragensis in Ponte Erectori Devotissimo
hrivincisa Eidem Prænobili Generoso et Consultissimo Viro oblata, data et dedicata
ab Quenthino Noiraulter, civæ Antiquo-
Urbensi et Calchographo ⟨...⟩

collected on the bridge and which from 1459 onwards went exclusively to the treasury of the Old Town through a decision of King Jiří of Poděbrady. This was no small tax, for it brought into the treasury of the town in the years 1433–1467 alone an average of 491 kop 34 gr. (the contemporary currency) yearly. A further source of income was derived from the proceeds of buildings dedicated to the upkeep of the bridge, and lastly there were also various private deeds giving money for this purpose. The Old Town privilege granted by King Jiří in 1459 was confirmed by King Vladislav Jagellon in 1472, and further strengthened by a decision of the same king in 1502 during a dispute of the Old Town with the gentry, who were refusing to pay the tolls. To commemorate their victory in the dispute the burghers of the Old Town erected the stone statue of Bruncvik on the tenth pillar of the bridge, as a visible symbol of their rights to the bridge. These rights were executed by special sentries and officials of the Prague bridge. Their offices on the left river bank which, although really on the territory of the Malá Strana came under the jurisdiction of the Old Town, were firstly in the Saxon House and later in the house No. 56-III on the bridge next to the lesser bridge tower, which was adapted for the office in 1591. On the right river bank the Office of the Bridge was housed in house No. 193-I, being that nearest to the Old Town bridge tower. The officials remained in this house until 1850, although the office itself was abolished in 1784. The upkeep of the bridge, that "precious and highly beneficial

---

13. *Ferdinand Max Brokoff*, St. Francis Borgia. 1710. Sandstone.

jewel of the city of Prague" as the scribe of the bridge office wrote in 1650, the bridge which was the subject of many verses and admiring remarks in the travel books of foreigners, was a lucrative undertaking for the burghers of the Old Town, in spite of the fact that the bridge had to be repaired and furnished with new decorations from time to time. An especially heavy expense was the repair of a demolished pillar and arch representing the stages of the cross (where the group "Piety" stands today) after the floods of 1496. This repair work dragged on until 1503, and it seemed so important in the minds of contemporaries that they erroneously connected the completion of the repairs with the conclusion of the whole bridge building. In 1591 the lesser Malá Strana tower was repaired and newly decorated. It was covered with rustic graffitos, new renaissance windows were built and also a new roof and gables. In the same year the old customs house below the tower was also rebuilt and decorated in the late renaissance style, and on its portal an inscription was carved recording the date and extent of this rebuilding. The increased building activities on the island of Kampa and the necessity of a direct access into the bridge from the island gave rise at the beginning of the 17th century to considerations as to how such a connection could be made. At the suggestion of the governor Karl of Lichtenštejn a project of a one-flight staircase next to the third or fourth pillar on the southern side of the bridge was prepared in 1622. The plans were worked out by the architect *Giovanni Campion de Bossi* and the

---

13a. A n g e l. A detail of Brokoff's group of St. Francis Borgia

carpenter *Giulio de Corni,* but for unknown reasons the project was not executed and it eventually disappeared into the official archives. It took more than one and a half centuries before that idea was again considered and finally carried out.

The bridge suffered severely in the summer and autumn of 1648, when the Swedish armies which had captured the Hradčany hill and Malá Strana. tried to conquer the Old Town. Across the narrow isthmus of the bridge the Swedes tried for three months to enter the quarter on the right bank, but they were always repelled. The Peace of Westphalia on November 6th 1648 put a sudden end to these attempts. Among the victims of the battles, besides many human lives, were also some statues from the bridge which, though not numerous at that time were therefore the more precious. The destruction of the sculptury on the western side of the Old Town tower was particularly regrettable, though identical figures now adorn the tower on the opposite side. There was a statue of the Madonna with the kneeling figures of Charles IV and his queen. During the repairs to the tower carried out in 1650–52 by the master-mason *Carlo Luragho* and stonemason *Giovanni Spinetti,* the remains of these plastics were removed and a marble slab with the description of the repairs was put up instead, at the cost of almost 5.000 gilders. At the same time a new group of statues, the Calvary, was erected in the place of some which had been destroyed during the battles.

In 1655 a certain amount of damage was caused to the bridge

III. This reproduction of *Werner's* drawing, published as part of a picture album of Prague memorials, emphasizes the new character of the bridge about 1740 after the erection of the statues, which are drawn with more care than artistry.

I. POHLED NA KARLU

by floods, but this had no serious consequences. Much more dangerous to the bridge were the floods of 1784 by which six pillars were damaged. There was a guard room on one of the pillars where stands today the statue of St. Christopher, and this guard room collapsed together with its staff, whose task it was to regulate the traffic on the bridge, and five soldiers perished. The repairs to the bridge after this catastrophe lasted four years, and were carried out by the Director of Land Buildings, František Leon. Herget, and the Director of Water Buildings, František Traxal, at a total cost of 152.325 gilders. The catastrophe had however one good side. It proved conclusively that the building of a staircase from the island of Kampa onto the bridge, which had been planned long before, was really necessary not only for communication for also for security reasons, to avoid the inhabitants of the island, which was constantly threatened by floods, from being forced in case of danger to climb to safety up ladders, as happened in 1784. Therefore a plain stone staircase was built in 1785, simplifying an old project of Gio. Campion's. This staircase was replaced in 1844 by the present doubleflight staircace in the new Gothic style, according to a project of the builder of St. Vitus Cathedral, *Josef Kranner*. In 1834–35 cast iron pavements made in the ironworks of Komárov were put onto the bridge for the safety of pedestrians threatened by the increasing horsedrawn traffic. Parts of these cast iron pavements were used by the Old Town students during the June revolution in 1848 to build a barricade, which they made inside the Old Town bridge tower to defend the quarter against the soldiers of Prince Windischgrätz in their suppression of the Prague citizens' revolt. Then, as two centuries before death and destruction passed across the bridge, and once again there were victims of the shooting amongst the statues on the bridge, which were seriously damaged by the missiles. Eight of the row of statues which had been put on the pillars of the bridge during the past two centuries through the piety and aesthetic and creative fervour of the culmination of the baroque epoch were so damaged that they had to be removed.

The new statues which were erected here in the years 1853–61 could not make good the losses of the battles in 1848. But it was not only the armed hand of man which destroyed the creative work of bygone generations, — the floods, a constant enemy and destroyer of the bridge, crashed with evil force against the artistic bequest of the baroque age and snatched from the alley of the bridge statues two of its most beautiful blossoms. On the 4th September 1890 the water damaged two of the bridge pillars, which collapsed. With them fell three arches and two of the most precious plastic groups of Ferdinand Max Brokoff, the statues of St. Ignace and St. Francis Xaverius. The damage caused by this catastrophe, which was felt throughout the cultural world, was repaired within two years by the building firm of Gregersen from Budapest under the direction of Ing. Jiří Soukup, at a cost of 665.600 crowns. But the loss of the statues was not and could never be made good, even when their remains were dredged out from the water some time later and placed in the national lapidarium.

14. *Josef Max,* St. Norbert with Ss. Wenceslas and Sigismund 1853. Sandstone.

III. THE SCULPTURES OF CHARLES BRIDGE.

The burghers of the Old Town made it their task to care for the decoration of the bridge with statues from the earliest times, urged on to do so by the custom of their time as well as by practical needs. It is thought that as early as Charles' times a cross was erected on the then unfinished bridge, and this is believed to have happened not long after 1361, to commemorate and condone for the fact that in that year the burghers of the Old Town illegally drowned a chaplain of St. Guy there. This cross probably stood on about the same place where there is a cross today, – the fourth successor to the original cross on the bridge. At some time during the 15th century there was built opposite to this cross, i. e. where the group of statues "Piety" stands today, a stage of the cross in the current form of a column surmounted by a miniature

---

14a. *Jan Brokoff*, St. Norbert with the beatified Adrian and James. Copperplate of Neuräutter's from a drawing by Karel Kulík from 1714. This group, which was built on the bridge in 1706, is untraceable.

B. Adrianus Martÿr

B. Iacobus Martÿr

GorCo=
MIenses
Præstan=
tes

EVCha=
rIstIæ
Defenso=
res

S. Norberti
MagDebVrgen=
LIs ArChI=
EpI=Cope=

Sect. MenlarIæ hæresIs
DebellLator
Ora pro Rege
et
Regno eIVs

Honori et Venerationi

Reverendissimi ac Illustrissimi Domini Domini VITI &c. et Apostolica sede Gratia Episcopi Hierosolitani, Archidiaecesi Gregensi Suffraganei, S.R.I.
Canonici et Prælati Ordinis Præmonstratensis celeberrimi Eremi, Strahoviensis Propositi Meritissimi, et Utriusque Status Regni &c.
Nobilis per Bohemiam Consortia Vicarii Generalis, et Visitatoris perpetui ac Ecclesiastici, Sui alee Regiae, Majestatis auxiliarii Honoris Veneratoris
mi, sui Patriarcha Norberti Propagatoris zelosissimi Omnium Patrem ac Mæcenatis Gratiosissimi.
A. Neuraitter cu. aut. Pri. Serg. objemissim. tertissimi vovet et consecrat.

Carol. Luka del. Ioan. Erckoff in Lezido elaboravit A. Neuraitter æri incidit

chapel. This column can still be seen in Sadeler's panorama of Prague of 1606. The first mention of it is in 1496, when part of the bridge next to it was destroyed by floods. The third statue to be built (some time after 1506) was the statue of Bruncvík mentioned earlier, the sign of the rights and might of the Old Town citizens on this bridge. Besides these three statues unconfirmed reports of later historians put forward the theory that the bridge was decorated with further statues, such as for instance, a statue of King Jiří of Poděbrady, which is said to have been destroyed by the soldiers of Passau in 1611; or the allegorical figure of Justice, and a heraldic figure of the Czech lion. But neither historical sources nor old illustrations of the bridge confirm the existence of such plastic ornamentation.

The three statues mentioned above were the sole decoration of the bridge for two centuries, that is up to the end of the 17th century. Only on the supposed anniversary of the torturing of St. Jan of Pomuk a new bronze statue of the newly created and revered patron of the country was built near to the place where the saint was supposedly thrown into the river. It was a work of some pretensions and was important in the artistic history of the bridge. Its patron, Matyáš Knight of Vunšvic spared no expense, even ordering a model in Vienna from the court sculptor *Mathias Rauchmüller*, and he had the statue and the relief on the pedestal cast in bronze in Nuremburg. What is important however is that he hereby created, though unconsciously, a local type of bridge deco-

---

14b. *Ignác Platzer senior,* St. Norbert and the angels. Copperplate of J. Salzer's from a drawing by Ign. Platzer. This group, which was built on the bridge in 1765, in place of Brokoff's group, is also untraceable.

PANIS VIVIFICI
NORBERTUS
CULTOR ET ULTOR
HINC
CELLIS OS CLAUDIT
SUB PEDIBUSQVE
RUIT.

Ignatius Platzer Statuarius et inv.   Salzer F. Scul Prage

VICTIMA NORBERTO PROSTABAT AB ANTE DICATA.   DEHINC LÆTA SION SIC RENOVAVIT EAM.

ration which was followed not only in the Czech lands but also far abroad, and which it appears was repeated not long afterwards, when other pillars of the Prague bridge were decorated with statues. Scarcely a decade after the erection of the statue of the former Queen's confessor, a further sculptural work arose on the bridge – Brokoff's group "Piety", which is a more complex composition and replaced the former Gothic column with the chapel. Shortly afterwards, some time during the last five years of the 17th century, *Ottavio Mosto* created, at the expense of Václav Markvart of Hradek, his counterpart to the statue of St. John, a group with the other patron saint of the nation, St. Wenceslas. This statue was later moved to the castle ramparts, where it stood between 1784–1906, and today rests in the lapidarium. And then, less than ten years later, Vunšvic's thought is further continued, and now more systematically. Between the years 1706–1714 seven of the foremost sculptural works of Prague took possession of the remaining pillars and changed its balustrade into a continuous and wonderful gallery of twenty-six statues, a stone alley of figures which is a real litany in stone to all the saints. Its fame was widely increased by Augustin Neureuter, who in 1714 published a folio of etchings of the bridge, and in 1715 the same thing in larger form. Also Kašpar Wussin and I. I. Kamenitzký helped considerably by their illustrated booklets to spread the knowledge of this Prague curiosity.

The idea of building plastic figures on bridge pillars arose from the spiritual sphere of Italian baroque. Its purest and best-known reali-

---

15. *Matyáš Braun*, St. Ludmila and St. Wenceslas. Circa 1720. Sandstone.

sation is the decoration of the Ponte dei Angeli in Rome, which was executed by the pupils of the founder of Roman baroque illusionism, Giovanni Lorenzo Bernini. It seems that this bridge was the direct example for the decoration of the Prague bridge, which is unequalled in the whole world for the number and complexity of its sculptural works. And this decoration was made at a time when the anti-Reformation movement, securing a hold in Bohemia, was basically changing mediaeval nordic Prague, in its buildings and its art, to be more like the towns of the Catholic area of southern Europe. The sculptural decoration of the Charles Bridge underline this artistic and ideological change of the capital of the state of Bohemia at the peak of the baroque period, and point to the victorious anti-Reformation. It is not known who gave the direct stimulus for the following of the examples set by Vunšvic and Markvart of Hradek and for the continuous realisation of statues and groups of statues on the Charles Bridge, but the speed of their execution and the placing according to one plan of some of these statues is both interesting and surprising. Examples of this are the groups of statues of St. Francis Xaverius and Ignacius de Loyola opposite one another over the midstream of the river, and the groups of Ss. Ivo and Kosma and Damian at either end of the bridge, all of which were built at the expense of the Jesuits of the University, then administered by Jesuits. All these show a preconceived plan of the placing of the statues, in which the most exposed places were reserved by the Jesuits. Other classes of the

15a. St. Ludmila and St. Wenceslas. A detail of Braun's group.

population competed for the remaining places: the nobles, church councils and townsmen, in agreement with the Prague District Council competed in founding memorials to the saints, as if to witness the sincerety of their religion and spirit of sacrifice, so that within less than a decade this magnificent and unique cycle was completed, which is important not only for the history of baroque sculpture in Bohemia, but in the whole of Central Europe. This could be achieved mainly owing to the participation of the two *Brokoffs*, the father *Jan* and the son *Ferdinand Max*, and of *Matyáš Braun*. Braun's share in the decoration of the bridge is small – Braun and his workshop carved for the bridge only the group of St. Luitgard and St. Ivon, and these were complemented later by that of St. Ludmila, which was brought from elsewhere. But for the history of the workshop of the Brokoff family, the statues built for the bridge are of great importance, not only because until the end of the first half of the last century, when part of their statues was replaced by newer creations of both *Maxes*, more than half of the statues on the bridge were their creations, but also because of the interesting relation between the works of Jan Brokoff and his son Ferdinand Max. Furthermore the statues give a remarkable proof of the artistic development of the younger Brokoff. After the creations of the old Jan Brokoff, that is after the model of St. John, which he carved from a sketch made by Rauchmüller in 1683, and after "Piety", 1695, which are without doubt entirely the work of this wood-engraver from Spiš, a man

---

15b. *Ottavio Mosto,* S t. W e n c e s l a s a n d t h e a n g e l s. Copperplate of Neuräutter's from a drawing of Karel Kulík's from 1714. This group, built on the bridge towards the end of the 17th century, is today partly in the country lapidarium (the statues) and on the Prague castle ramparts (the pedestal).

Illustrissimo Domino Domino Wenceslao Ernesto Marquard de Hradek, Domino in Werne,
dieser ist Frauder, J. C. Re: Ma: Consiliario, Camerario, Regii Conventionis Hagero, Judicii Provincialis Assessori,
nec non Regis sub cancellarii in Regno Bohemia, Domino ac Patrono suo Observand: mo: Hic Dei Bohemiæ Judicibus, ac Patriæ
Patriæ Principis sanctorum prototypi, ac sanctitatis idea, Wenceslai in Ponte Prageno: no: Illmæ Dominationis suæ mu:
nifica liberalitate in vagina vero chalcographicæ obsequissimi scalptoris opera, procuratur & octupo, perpetuæ
observantiæ testeram, dicat, dedicat, consecrat.   Illustriss: mæ Dominationis suæ
                                                                    Aug: Heinmüller invent: & Sculpsit Pet: Prag: io

without imagination and an unskilled stonemason, there follow two works, the baptism of Christ and St. Joseph from 1706, where these deficiencies of Jan's art are softened by a greater certainty in the chisel work. There is no doubt that the hand that wielded this chisel belonged to the son, Ferdinand Max. The art of the young Brokoff showed itself still more freely however, in the three groups which were contracted by Brokoff's workshop towards the end of the first decade of 18th century. The group of St. Barbara with s. Katherine and Elisabeth from 1708 is, in its lively modelling and plastic fulness, the first free expression of a new spirit in the Brokoff workshop, and this is seen to an even greater extent in the works of the following two years, when the statues of St. Kajetan (1709), and of St. Francis Borgia (1710) achieve the level of quite independent works of art. But it is only in the groups of St. Francis Xaverius, St. Ignacius. St. John of Matha, and in the statue of St. Guy, finished in the years 1711–1714, that the young Brokoff achieves complete independence of exposition as well as of execution. This differentiation of the work of the two Brokoffs is based only on stylisric differences, and is not either founded on historic proofs nor shown by the signatures to the statues, which uniformly show only the name of Jan Brokoff as the owner of the workshop, but not as the real author of the work. However, his own statues can easily be distinguished from the work done by his son. The work of Jan Brokoff is rooted deeply in the tradition of the 17th century, and one sees his training as a wood engraver

---

16. *Mathias Rauchmüller*, St. John of Nepomuk. 1683. Bronze.

even when he attempts to put new feeling into his work. The triple system of the composition, its exact symmetry, which is heightened in his figures to a mirror-like reflection of the same gesture from one side to the other, the stiff modelling, the lack of conviction in the movements, the strengthening of the pedestal by a protruding cornice, and his shallow attempts to liven his figures up by repetition of the stereotyped leaf-motive, the interlocking of single parts, and their obvious disjointedness: such are the signs of the work of the old Brokoff. These peculiarities are fundamentally present also in the work actually done by the young Brokoff too, but here the conception of the types, which are full of life and passion, perfectly modelled in form as well as in their anatomically correct movements, and which are presented in excited attitudes and gestures, easily surpasses the older Brokoff's conception. These figures also gain especially by the soft folds of the draperies, arranged without hesitation, which heighten with monumental effect the sense and importance of the statues. Even where both are working together one can see the difference of the two hands. In the group of Christ's Baptism St. John the Baptist is reminiscent of the "Piety" in the stiffness of his expression and the rigidity of his muscles. But the Christ clearly shows those signs which were already becoming characteristic of the work of the son. With the passage of time, the son's co-operation in the figures on the bridge grows until he becomes completely independent. In the last group of statues of St. Francis Borgia, which is still basically dependent on the father's

---

IV. This carefully drawn document of J. Gregory's is an objective record of the state of the bridge towards the end of the 18th century, which evidently was not very different from that of today. In detail however, we can see here the outlines of the numerous statues which were later replaced by works of the two Maxes.

IV. POHLED NA

conception, F. M. Brokoff definitely disregards symmetry, and in later
works which are exclusively his own he discards even the architecto-
nically arranged pedestals. He either transforms them into figural
supports portraying figures ideologically connected with the fate of
the saint, such as for instance in the case of Ss. Xaverius, Ignacius
de Loyola and St. Prokop, where the defeated are carrying the
saint as a victor, or he even goes so far as to show on the pedestal
the whole story of the legend, as in the case of St. Guy and
the group with St. Evan. Here the young Brokoff even surpasses
Matyáš Braun, who persists in the use of architectonical pedestals
for his statues. Here too the individualities of these two sculptors
are distinguishable, their paths divide. The young Brokoff's development is more aggressive, he is not afraid of consequences, because his spirit is not curbed by any important school of tradition.
He learnt his art only from his father, was probably never in Italy,
and is reputed to be almost a self-made man, although some of his
motives, in particular the plastic conception of his pedestals, show
beyond doubt that he knew of the contemporary sculpture abroad, especially in Salzburg. Braun, on the other hand, is a pupil
of Bernini's Roman school, and also often co-operates with an
architect. His conception is therefore more disciplined and he has
a greater sense for the architectural side of the work. Where for
instance, the young Brokoff places the balcony on the facade of
the Morzin Palace in the Malá Strana directly on the shoulders
of the Moors, Braun sees in the giants of the Clam-Gallas or the
eagles of the Thun Palace an animated column or pillar, which
cannot be connected with its burden without an intermediary link.
He therefore places on their heads the crown of a column or some
similar link. This consistency, which reminds one rather of an architect, can also be observed in his works on the bridge. Their pedestals hardly seem the work of a sculptor, and were almost certainly projected by an architect, perhaps Braun's best friend, F. M.
Kaňka. The sculptural work grows from these pedestals in a flowing
and easy form and conception which remind one of Italy. St. Luit-

this he is the pioneer of highly developed baroque in our country. Mosto's influence on Brokoff can be seen in the latter's plastic conception of the pedestal, as exemplified in the Mirabell, in Salzburg where, twenty years before Brokoff, Mosto had invented a method of showing on the pedestal the meaning of the statue itself.

Hand in hand with Mosto as regards the tendency of his work, though not the level of achievement, goes *Matěj Václav Jäkl,* of Saxon origin, who carved for the bridge the statue of St. Anne and the two groups of statues, St. Bernard and St. Dominic with Thomas Aquinas. The works of this sculptor's maturity, although of a clear style, lack the purity and bearing of Octavian's work. It is as if the artist was able to express only half of what he wished to convey. As one of the school of Roman sculptural illusionism, Jäkl knows how to achieve a picturesque composition of his groups, he lends a vivid expression of pathetic feeling to his figures, but he is unable to breath into them that dynamism that consists of convincing action of the body and of garments tossed by the wind. The garments of Jäkl's figures on the bridge are rigid, as if weighted by the fall of their angular and sharply broken folds, and recall the long-forgotten style of the late Gothic wood engravers.

These two, Mosto and Jäkl, represent on the bridge, together with Braun, the extreme tendency in the baroque sculpture of the 18th century – sculptural illusionism. Their aim was no longer the rendering of objective reality, but of the highest aim of the baroque spirit, an objective expression of a complicated state of mind,

17. *Emanuel Max,* St. Francis Seraphim with the angels. 1855. Sandstone.

a petrifaction of the manifestations of life and passionate feeling in plastic form.

The other contributors to the decoration of the bridge were much more sober both in their plastic aims and in their means. *František Preiss*, a wood engraver and innkeeper of Hradčany, is, according to the monogram F. P., in Kamenitzky's description of the statues the author of the group of St. Francis Seraphim, which today stands in front of the Capucin church in Revoluční náměstí. Preiss is a supporter of the traditional Czech monumental realism. He is a skilful modeller and a first class stonemason, and in this he is the predecessor of the younger Brokoff. The bodies of his figures are composed of parts observed separately, and show a quiet pathos clothed in dignified and heavy monumentality. In this he is more advanced than an artist of the same kind, *Jan Oldřich Mayer*, an Austrian, who created the statues of Ss. Antonín and Juda for the bridge, and also the group of Ss. Kosma and Damian. His short-bodied figures are ill-formed even for their period, and their lack of expression again shows the wood carver who is unable to possess the stone and force his will upon it. He merely worked upon the surface of the block, unable to penetrate its depth or to develop from it more eloquent attitudes or gestures, and still less the movement of drapery. In short his characteristics are in all details those conventional of sculptors of the 17th century. An incomparably greater sculptor in this direction is Mayer's contemporary *Jan Bedřich Kohl*, who in 1708 added to the bridge

---

17a. *František Preiss*, St. Francis Seraphim. Copperplate of Neuräutter's from a drawing of Karel Kulík's from 1714. The statues of the group, built on the bridge in 1708, are today in front of the church of St. Joseph in Prague II.

PATRI ARCHA SERA PHICE ORA PRO NOBIS DEVM

S. FRANCISCUS

Pauper modus
profeditur
cœlum dives
ingreditur.

Christi Stigmata Ordinis Insignia.

Ordo Dei Magno Ordo Trivm Phat.

Carl: Bitlich del.

Aug: Heiucracher sculp.

Admodum Reverende ac Religiosissime Patri in Christo Patri Placido Inclyti ac Cœle
berrimi Ordinis Cappucinorum per Provinciam Bohemiæ Ministro Provinciali dignissimo nunc hic Chrysostomo, qui singulari desiderio, ac terreno triumphans, mollia gloriam venerantur, quam in Orbe Patri in Christo etc etc. accusando, operariorum Dominus Æternum Asymptotus, cætera pauper et humilis, cuius dis re integrity e Si Vng Patriæ ac Patriarchæ Seraphici, ostendi e Sancte Aragonis ad hanc veggin a Authario quoto ad hoc chalcographiæ in cuius in suo cordis Ordinis officiorum me-
rumentum, transtulit. S. D.
Suscipe tibi felici ac Cœli ma Æternitati
obsequentiss: mé Aug: Heiucracher.

the statues of St. Augustin and St. Michael Tolentine. He was one of the sculptors who were not hampered by the technique of the wood engraver. He understood the peculiar properties of stone and left them as such without violation. For this reason his statues possess a plastic fulness, softness and roundness, particularly in the garments. By the rich folds of their draperies he greatly increases the monumental effect of his figures, which make the other statues on the bridge look mild and moderate in their expressions of passion. These draperies are broadly cast and are logically connected with the actions of the body, thus combining dignity with eloquence.

The integral work of the baroque statues on the Charles Bridge ends with the work of a sculptor more significant than all the others, although he is not of the same generation as our artists of the 18th century. This is the statue of St. Philip Benitius from 1714 by *Michal Bernard Mandl*, sculptor from Salzburg. Mandl, who is said to be Czech by origin, is one of greatest individualities of Austrian baroque. His artistic fate was shaped by a fruitful cooperation with the outstanding Central European architect of that time, Johann B. Fischer von Erlach. The number and standard of their joint works far surpassed that of their Austrian contemporaries. Starting as a representative of Roman sculptural illusionism, Mandl developed in his maturity the expression of calm monumentality, which is perfectly embodied in his Charles Bridge statue. This is the last of Mandl's known works, and is also interesting for the

---

18. *Jan Oldřich Mayer*, St. Anthony of Padua. 1707. Sandstone.

fact that, as distinct trom the other statues on the bridge, which are of sandstone, it is carried out in Salzburg marble. Unlike the earlier ecstatic and moving figures of this sculptor, St. Philip is portrayed in a calm and composed attitude. The ecstasy of baroque is concentrated in his enraptured gaze, and the spiritual content of the work confined to an inner spiritual tension which penetrates the whole figure, the gestures and even the meticulously and simply modelled draperies. In its whole conception this statue foretells the future development in sculpture, which came remarkably soon, towards the later baroque classic idealism. With the statue of St. Philip, which was created in Salzburg itself, the baroque sculptural work of the bridge ends. The later phase of the 18th century had little to add to it. In 1764 a new group of St. Norbert and the angels was erected in place of Brokoff's group, which got broken. This new group was carved by the leading sculptor of Prague rococo, *Ignác Platzer*, and it had all the softness and flexibility and also the characteristic flatness of all Platzer's rococo sculptury. And some twenty years later the statue of St. Wenceslas by O. Mosto was damaged by floods, and in its place a statue of St. Ludmila was erected, brought here from an unknown source. This work, which does not bear the signs used by *Matyáš Braun*, belongs stylistically to the third decade of the 18th century. Both these statues, carried out in the baroque spirit are incorporated organically into the bridge as an artistic whole and harmoniously fill the empty spaces over the two pillars.

---

19. *Ferdinand Max Brokoff*, St. Vincent of Ferrara and St. Prokop. 1712. Sandstone.

But in the 19th century it was a different matter. Bourdelle called Charles Bridge "the centaur" – a horse below, a man above, the whole composed of two irreconcilable styles. The massive Gothic horizontal building carries a whole connected row of vertical statues which undulate like stone flowers, enlivening and breaking its heavy outlines. Unfortunately this series of figures has long lost its original unity of artistic form. The twentieth century, with its practicalness and historico-scientific attitude to architectural monuments interrupted the artistic integrity of this uniformly planned and built work of art. If practical needs which are today acknowledged have reconciled us to this fact, together with the tact of the architect Josef Kranner, who built the two-flight neogothic stairway down to Kampa on the southern side of the bridge, nothing can repair the offence to the sight caused by the breaking-up of the series of baroque statues. It is of no help to be resigned to the damage caused by natural disasters, nor to acknowledge objectively that the period which completed the series of plastic works could not have built them otherwise than it did.

Owing to the damage to the bridge by the floods of 1784 and even more those of 1890, and also owing to the shooting on the bridge in the year of revolution 1848, part of the baroque statues were either destroyed or so much damaged that they had to be removed. Some statues were re-erected elsewhere, such as Brokoff's group "Pieta" which stands today in the hospital garden of the Sisters of Mercy under Petřín hill, or St. Francis Seraphim which

---

19a. A J e w. A detail of Brokoff's group of St. Vincent of Ferrara and St. Prokop.

is now in the niche on the wall in front of the church of St. Joseph in the Capucin convent; the majority however were pieced together and laid in the country lapidarium in Stromovka gardens. In their stead new and almost similar statues were erected, but these were of course new in their style and artistic conception, and often diametrically opposed to the baroque conception of the unity of the whole. Most of the statues had already been replaced by new ones by about the first half of the last century, and these, with one exception, were composed and worked out without any regard to their surroundings. This one exception is the group of St. Cyril and Methodius by *Karel Dvořák*, which was built in 1938 on the occasion of the anniversary of the independent Czechoslovak Republic, and replaced the former group of St. Ignacius, which was damaged. Its author succeeded in fittingly placing a modern work next to those of his baroque predecessors. But the authors of the other new statues, *Josef* and *Emanuel Max*, and their fellow-worker *Josef Kamil Böhm*, adhered to an artistic conception which was quite contrary to the baroque aesthetics of the rest of the statues on the bridge. Their academic principles and their conservative classical vision of art, which was full of the schematic feeling of the German nazarenism, appearing particularly in plastic and linear form, brought forth nothing but lifeless symbols of unreal types and harsh expression. At the time of their creation the works of the Maxes were considered as far surpassing the value of the original baroque decorations to the bridge. However,

---

19b. *Ludvík Šimek*, B r u n c v í k. 1884. Sandstone.

today's criticism sees in them an impoverishment and devaluation of an eminent building monument, the proof of an artistically stagnant and poor period when, as a substitute for independent and individualistic expression based on a clear spiritual outlook, artists fell back on historical retrospection and exploitation of the past. This can be seen most clearly on the pedestals of these unimaginative statues, which are mostly combined of Gothic motives, but whose authors did not hesitate to use elements of the then defamed baroque to heighten their effect.

Charles Bridge as a whole is a live and illustrative picture of the ups and downs of the town over a period of five and a half centuries. Truly history has moved through its gates, the bridge has lived through events both magnificent and melancholic, over it have passed processions to coronations and other great events, funerals, and armies bringing the destruction of war. But here also everyday life has flowed, with its daily bustle, with its everchanging forms and figures. Many pictures, from a woodcut of 1562 to works of modern masters and photographers, show us how the surroundings of the bridge were changing, they show us tens of generations for whom the bridge was a link between the two banks of Prague. For a time, in 1890, the bridge was out of working order owing to severe damage, but modern technique buickly repaired it and made it secure for a long time to come. Soon afterwards however, it was again threatened, this time by the thoughtlessness of the city's administrators, who wanted it

---

V. The second part of J. Gregory's panorama of the banks of Prague shows the bridge from the opposite side from the foregoing one. Here the original baroque integrity of the sculptural decoration is even more evident. In the foreground, where the military guardhouse stood until 1784 is a pedestal with the tablet which is today on the side of the tower. In the background are the groups of the Lord's Christening and St. Ignác.

used for a tramline. Mercifully they were prevented from carrying out the barbaric project of putting posts for the tram trolleys in between the statues, and the whole project was abandoned. Without failing in its centuries-old service to the inhabitants of Prague, the bridge keeps on the whole, even in modern times, its integrity which was founded in the Gothic and fulfilled in the baroque age. The fact that the transport of heavy vehicles across the bridge is forbidden, and that the bridge itself is under constant supervision, guarantees for it further life and an old age which is not despised but respected, an old age not of passive rest but actively helping in every way it can towards the further development of the town in its ever more complicated and richer life.

IV. GUIDE TO CHARLES BRIDGE.

The approach to the bridge, originally called the Stone Bridge and also the Prague Bridge, and since 1870 officially known as Charles Bridge, is formed on the Old Town side by the small Křižovnický Square, originally called Bridge Square, but today named after the Convent of the Cross (Křižovnický klášter) which forms the whole of the northern side of the square. The square as it stands today is the work of the brothers Klein from 1846–1848, and was carried out as a connected whole with the founding of the memorial to the Emperor Charles IV. When it was built the military guardhouse which stood to the north of the entrance to the bridge was demolished—a simple one-storey building from the 17th century, and also the so-called Vintner's Column with its statue of St. Wenceslas carved by *Jan Jiří Bendl* in 1676, which ori-

---

20. *Jan Oldřich Mayer*, St. J u d a T a d e a s. 1708. Sandstone.

ginally stood in front of the guardhouse in the middle of the traffic route, was removed from where it stood since 1778, at the southeastern corner of the guardhouse. After the guardhouse's demolition the column was transferred to its present position at the corner of the Church of the Cross (kostel křižovníků). When the guardhouse was demolished the question of the enlargement of the terrain of the square to the west was solved by arching over an arm of the Vltava, so that it flowed under the Convent of the Cross, and by enlarging the space between the first pillars of the bridge and the bridge tower and the main Convent building. Thus the former arch and two pillars of the Judith Bridge were covered by this main building, as can be seen from the illustration in Weleba's book "Die berühmte Prager Brücke" from 1827. At the same time the carved stone head of the so-called "Bearded Man", which had at one time been set in the arch of the Judith Bridge, was placed on the wall of the new embankment. In the newly formed square was erected the cast iron memorial to Charles IV, cast in the works of J. Burgschmid in Nurenburg (the figure of the Emperor) and in Saxony (the pedestal with the allegorical figures of the four faculties), at the expense of Charles University, according to the model of the Dresden sculptor Ernst Hähnel. The northern wall of the square behind the memorial is formed by the main building of the Convent of the Cross, which still remains today in the imitation early baroque style as it was built by *Carlo Luragho* towards the end of the 17th century. The former romanesque en-

---

21. *Jan Bedřich Kohl,* St. Michael Tolentine. 1708. Sandstone.

trance to the Judith Bridge tower was joined onto this building, and gave it the apperance of a deep salient which at the south-western corner of the building rises in the direction of the Old Town bridge tower. The top floor of the main building was added in 1847 at the wish of the Grand-Master Jakub Beer. The rest of this side of the square is closed in by the Church of the Cross, consecrated to St. Francis Seraphim, and built in the years 1680–89 on the site of the original early Gothic church from the middle of the 13th century according to a project of the French architect *Jean B. Mathey.* The front of the church – a remarkably noble building in the classic Roman style, with a central cupola – is richly decorated with statues from various sources. The two statues on the ground floor of the Virgin Mary and St. John Nepomuk from 1756 are probably the work of the Prague sculptor *Richard Prachner,* while the statues in the niches on the facade, portraying the patron saint of the church and the Czech patron saints are probably by *Filip O. Quitainer* and date from the beginning of the 18th century. The angels surmounting the eaves came from the workshop of *Matěj V. Jäkl* in 1722. The interior of the church, decorated with wall frescos of the Last Judgement by V. V. Reiner from 1723, is remarkable for its rich woodwork, altars, statues from the workshops of M. V. Jäkl and the *Süssner brothers,* and altar cloths made by *Michal Willmann* at the beginning of the 18th century. The eastern side of the square is walled by the Church of St. Saviour, formerly the main

---

22. *Jan Bedřich Kohl*, St. Augustine. 1708. Sandstone.

church of the Order of the Jesuits in Prague. In style this church is a mixture of the elements of late renaissance and early baroque, gradually pieced together, built onto and redecorated since 1578 to 1657, when the beautiful portico of the church with the statues of the Madonna and the Church Fathers was built by *Jan Jiří Bendl* after Florentine models round the buildings of Cigoli. Next to this portico a part of the Klementinum also looks onto the square. This was originally the main Prague college of the Jesuits, and is today the National and University Library. Its portal, built about 1660 is probably from a project of the Italian architect *Domenico Orsi*, and the votive tablet of Josef II is by the Prague builder *Ignác Palliardi* from 1783. On the southern side the square is bordered by three private buildings. From Charles Street (Karlova ulice) part of the former Mansfeld Palace No. 189 – an ostentatious baroque building from 1735 – juts out to the square. The second house, No. 194, has a subway onto the former street, and was rebuilt in late Empire style, reminding one of 1405. It is not otherwise particularly interesting. As for the third building, No. 193, the one nearest to the bridge, ornamented on the corner by a relief of the imperial eagle, this is a house of historic importance. It used to be the seat of the office of Vinegrowers, which was founded in 1358 by Charles IV, and abolished by Josef II in 1783. Its task was to administer the Prague vineyards, which were at one time on almost all the sunny slopes around Prague, and to look after them. The house was built on the site of the former toll house in the

---

23. *Matyáš Bernard Braun*, St. Luitgarde. 1710. Sandstone.

time of Rudolf II, about 1600. It used to be a showy late renaissance building, rich with pilasters and coats-of-arms, and with a decorated marble portal. In 1855 it was rebuilt in the sober form in which we see it today. The coats-of-arms have been taken down or destroyed, the portal transferred to the Old Town Hall. The fourth, the western side of Křižovnický square is formed partly by a short embankment with a pseudo-Gothic cast iron balustrade from the middle of the 19th century, and partly by the entrance to the bridge. This leads to the gate of the Old Town bridge tower, which stands for strategic reasons on the first pillar of the bridge. This tower, one of the noblest of the Prague Gothic buildings and undoubtedly one of the most beautiful memorials of the European Middle Ages, was founded at the same time as the bridge in 1357, according to a plan of *Peter Parler's*, and finished at the beginning of the 15th century. It was then restored in 1874—8 by Josef Mocker, and is today a two-storied prism with a pinnacle and a high sloping slate roof. On the southern side there is a built-on staircase the height of the tower with its pyramid-form roof. On the ground floor the gate takes the whole width, with its pointed arches and archivolts, bordered with figures and upheld with carved cornices, and inside it is vaulted into a star-shaped groined arch bolted with a crown. The ornamentation is in part still the original work, done by *Peter Maixner*, in 1877, the restored and repainted frescos of Veraikon with the angels, a picture of a light woman, the emblem of the kingfisher in a wreath and the coat-of-arms

---

23a. St. Luitgarde. Detail of Braun's statue.

of the empire and of the city of Prague. Over the arch of the gate facing the square are carved emblems in relief of Václav IV, pictures of the kingfisher in a frame formed by a circle of twisted veil, and a belt of the ten emblems of those countries which, in the second half of the 14th century, pertained to the Czech crown. These are, from the centre to the right: the imperial eagle, the eagless of Moravia, Svídnice (Schweidnitz) and Vratislava (Breslau), and the lily of Nise (Neisse); and to the left: the Czech lion, the lion of Luxemburg, and coats-of-arms of Zhořelec, Budišín and Lower Lusatia. Reckoning by the dates at which some of these countries belonged to the Czech crown, these emblems and the part of the tower on which they are placed must have originated in the years 1373—1377. The most remarkable and beautiful part of the tower's decoration is however on the eastern side on the first floor. The ingenious combination of odd arcades is here developed with the pointed motive of the ground floor of the tower. In the central arcade on the cornice under the canopy are placed statues of the builders of the bridge, Charles IV and Václav IV. These are the most perfect plastic portraits of the whole of Central European Gothic sculpture, and witness the high standard of Parler's art and the maturity of his stone-works. Judging by the appearance of Václav IV (born 1361) these statues must have been carved in the eighties of the 14th century. In the middle, between the two emperors there stands on a pedestal, in composition similar to two arches of the bridge, the statue of St. Guy. At the sides are the emblems

---

24. *Ferdinand Max Brokoff*, St. Gaetano. 1709. Sandstone.

of the Roman Empire and the Kingdom of Bohemia, and over St. Guy is the flaming eagle of St. Wenceslas. The second storey of the tower is decorated with eight double panelled arcades. In the flat surface of the two central lower arcades are statues of St. Adalberf and St. Sigismund, also from Parler's workshop. At the corners of the tower are flying buttress pillars, upheld by cornices portraying male and female figures, treated in the contemporary spirit of drollery.

The western side of the tower, facing the bridge, is decorated in the same way as the eastern side. During the battles with the Swedes in 1648 the ornamentation of the first floor on this side was so severely damaged that it had to be removed. According to old illustrations, of which the most exact is that in Sadeler's prospect of 1606, the architectural arrangement here used to be the same as that on the other side, and the analogous plastic decoration shows a standing figure of the Madonna in the middle and on either side of her kneeling figures of the Emperor (most probably Charles IV) and the Empress. During the repair work carried out after 1648 under the directions of Carl Luragho, a marble memorial tablet of Giovanni Spinetti's was placed here with a gilded engraved Latin inscription recording the repairs to this side of the tower in the reign of Ferdinand III, in the years 1650–52. Of the original decorations the only ones which remained on this side were the emblem of the kingfisher in the circle of veil and the coats–of–arms of Arelat and Austria.

---

25. *Josef Michal Brokoff?* St. Adalbert. 1709. Sandstone.

There is another tablet on the ground floor on the northern side of the tower, looking towards the Convent of the Cross. It formerly stood on the pillar which is today surmounted by the statue of St. Christopher. The inscription here records repairs to the bridge after the floods of 1784, carried out in the time of Josef II. The tablet was moved to its present position in 1857. Inside the tower there is one room on each floor, with timbered ceilings which were restored in 1878. At the end of the spiral staircase is a statue of a steward with the keys. Under the paving of the gate are two cellars, one under the other, which were formerly used as prison cells for debtors.

25a. Cherub. A detail from the pedestal of Brokoff's statue of St. Adalbert.

THE PLASTIC DECORATION OF THE BRIDGE PILLARS
going from the Old Town to Malá Strana.

LEFT SIDE.

1. The group of St. Ivon. (Sandstone from Hořice.)
1908, a copy of *Fr. Hergesel's* after the original of *Matyáš Braun* from 1711. Builder: Faculty of Law of Charles University in Prague.

The original of this group is in the country lapidarium in Prague. The statues show an open group which symbolises the specific quality of the saint as a spiritual judge who helped the socially weak against the injustice of the mighty. Behind the figure of St. Ivon there is a group consisting of an

RIGHT SIDE.

2. The group of St. Bernard. (Sandstone.)
1709. – Sculptor: *Matěj Václav Jäkl.*
Builder: Benedikt Littwerig, Abbot of the Cistercian Monastery in Osek.

On the asymmetrical three-part pedestal there is a group of the kneeling St. Bernard, founder of the Order of the Cistercians, adoring the Madonna. Below the Madonna and on the left are angels holding the Abbot's mitre and the emblems of the suffering of Christ, which are also the symbolic attributes of the saint. (For the inscription which

---

26. *Michal Bernard Mandl*, St. Philip Benitius. 1714. Marble.

old man and a mother and child, and on the other side the allegorical figure of Justice. The relief on the pedestal shows the mass of St. Ivon being celebrated on the settlement of a dispute between a mother and her son.

3. The group of St. Barbara, St. Margaret and St. Elizabeth. (Sandstone.)
1707.–Sculptor: *Ferdinand Max Brokoff.*
Builder: Jan Václav Obytecký of Obytec, Imperial Councillor and assessor of the County Court.

There are three isolated figures on a richly developed three-part pedestal which is decorated with a highly raised akant and ornamental bows and cartouches engraved with the emblems of the sculptor. St. Barbara is in the middle, St. Elizabeth on the right and St. Margaret on the left. Under St. Barbara's foot is the signature of Jan Brokoff as the owner of the sculptury works. The standard of the sculptures however shows a greater ability than we associate with the name of Jan Brokoff, and therefore we must assume that this is the oldest independent work of his son, Ferdinand Max.

is carved on this group, and on the other statues, turn to the special section on inscriptions.)

4. The group of St. Thomas Aquinas and St. Dominic. (Sandstone.)
1708. – Sculptor: *Matěj Václav Jäkl.*
Builder: The Dominican Convent of St. Giles of Prague Old Town.

This group, on its symmetrical three-part pedestal with inscribed scrolls, is composed into an equilateral triangle. The central axis is formed by the statue of the Madonna and Jesus, giving a rosary to St. Dominic, the founder of the Dominican Order (founded in the 13th century), who is kneeling on the left part of the pedestal surrounded by emblems of his rank (Abbot's mitre and statue of a dog carrying a torch, the emblem of the Order). On the right, symmetrical with St. Dominic, stands St. Thomas Aquinas, after the founder the most important member of the Order, an outstanding philosopher and creator of a school of philosophy. Books, a quill, a chain with the shining

---

27. *Ferdinand Max Brokoff,* St. John of Matha, St. Felix of Valois and St. Evan. 1704. Sandstone.

sun and an angel holding a beehive are the symbols showing his personal qualities and historical importance.

5. The group of Piety. (Sandstone.) 1859. – Sculptor: *Emanuel Max.* Builder: The City of Prague, from public donations.

The group shows the Virgin Mary and St. Magdalene bemoaning the death of Christ, and above them St. John Evangelist. Over the whole group there towers an empty crucifix.

A cross of perhaps similar form, i. e. a column with a pyramidical summit, stood on this site as early as the 15th century, as we see in Sadeler's picture from 1606. This was however destroyed during the floods of 1496, when the bridge pillar under it collapsed. In 1695 the group of Piety by *Jan Brokoff* was erected in its place. This group of statues was transferred in 1859 to the garden of the Convent of the Sisters of Mercy under the Petřín hill, where it still stands. The present group was built by Max in its place.

6. Group of the Calvary. (Sandstone.)

In origin and style this is an unequal group. The bronze gilded body of Christ was bought in 1657 at the cost of 500 tolars from the merchants Hillinger of Dresden. The Hebrew inscription of the same material from 1696 was acquired from the fine paid by a Jew who mocked at the cross. The cartouches on the pedestal of the cross, containing an inscription in three languages about this incident, are the work of an anonymous sculptor, signing himself GH, and date from 1707. The marble balustrade of the bridge under this group dates from 1681. The coat-of-arms of the nobles of Říčany and the Latin inscription on the border are in memory of a gift of Karl Adam Lev's of Říčany from 1672, when he bequeathed the estates of Louňovice and Vodlochovice to the Prague archbishopric on condition that they kept an eternal light burning under the cross.

The sandstone statue of the Virgin

27a. A Turk. A detail from the pedestal of Brokoff's group of St. John of Matha, St. Felix of Valois and St. Evan.

Mary and St. John Evangelist, 1861. –
Sculptor: *Emanuel Max*. The original
cross was built here not long after 1361
by a Prague magistrate. This is said to
have been destroyed by the Hussites in
1419. A new cross was put up some
time in the second half of the 15th century. In 1629 a new cross was acquired
with a wooden corpus and three figures: the Virgin Mary, St. John and St.
Mary Magdalene, painted òn wood. In
1648 this group was destroyed by the
shooting in the battles between the
citizens of Prague and the Swedes. The
head of Christ was, however, saved,
and this is today in the Prague Archbishop's Seminary. A further portrayal
of the Calvary was built on the bridge,
with two statues under the cross which
were carved from wood by *Jeremiáš
Fischel* and painted by *Fabián Harovník*.
As in 1657 this group became considerably decayed, the present metal corpus
was bought from fines which had to be
paid by Bohuchval Valkoun of Adlar,
a noble of Zlonice. In place of Fischel's
and Harovník's wooden figure two
leaden statues were put under the cross
in 1666, cast by the Prague bell-founder
Mikuláš Löw of Löwenberg. These

27b. Imprisoned christians. A detail from the pedestal of the group
of St. John of Matha, St. Felix and St. Evan.

pieced together by the sculptor Vosmík. Today it is in the country lapidarium in Prague. It represents an open group of East Indian and Japanese noblemen who were baptised by the saint, and whose bodies form a pedestal for the statue of St. Francis, holding aloft a cross before which the Indian princes and pages kneel, about to receive the sacrament.

On the back of the statue of one of the nobles is the signature of Jan Brokoff as the owner of the workshop. This group, in its composition and modelling, is one of the most remarkable of the statues on the Charles Bridge.

in Prague VII. This group was carved in 1711 by *Ferdinand Max Brokoff*, at the expense of the Jesuit convent of St. Ignacius of Prague New Town. When the bridge was damaged by floods in 1890 this group fell into the water, and had to be dragged out twice in that year and again in 1904; it was then pieced together by the sculptor Vosmík. It represents the founder of the Jesuit Order in an ecstatic pose as a priest, dressed in a cassock with a monstrance in his hand, standing on a globe which is supported by allegorical figures of the four then known continent. The weapons and military instruments symbolise the saint's activities before his spiritual awakening at the Battle of Pampelon. – A wooden model of Brokoff's statue is in the City of Prague collection.

11. The group of St. Christopher. (Sandstone.)
1857. – Sculptor: *Emanuel Max*.
Builder: Václav Wanka, a Mayor of Prague.

On a prismatic pedestal with twisted spiral columns in the late Gothic style, there is the figure of the saint in a ty-

12. Group of St. John the Baptist. (Sandstone.)
1857. – Sculptor: *Josef Max*.
Builder: Jan Norbert Gemerich of Neuberg.

On an architectonical pedestal with the coat-of-arms of the builder, the saint stands giving his blessing.

---

29. *Josef Kamil Böhm*, St. Wenceslas. 1858. Sandstone.

disfavour of the Emperor's representative in Bohemia and the lack of interest of the Emperor himself. It seems that the marble statue of the Emperor Charles VI, which today stands in the Laxenburg castle in Vienna was to have been part of this group, and the fact that the project was not completed has robbed the bridge of a work which would have been extraordinary from the point of view of its contents as well as artistically.

13. Group of St. Francis Borgia. (Sandstone.)

1710.— Sculptor: *Ferdinand Max Brokoff*. Builder: František of Collet, Imperial burgrave and taxcollector in Vienna New Town.

This is a noble composition in triangular form on a richly developed and ornamented base with the personal emblems of the saint, the third general of the Jesuits. The saint, with the appurtenances of his Jesuitical rank, is portrayed in a state of spiritual uplift, with the figures of two angels holding his saintly attributes. On the cordon at the left, near one of the angel's feet is the signature of Jan Brokoff, which

of the bridge a cast bronze tablet with a relief of St. John lying on the waves. This marks the place where the saint is supposed to have been thrown into the Vltava. This tablet from the 18th century is decorated with a rolled frame dating from the 19th century.

14. The group of St. Norbert, St. Wenceslas and St. Sigismund. (Sandstone.)

1853.— Sculptor: *Josef Max*. Builder: The Strahov Abbot Dr. Jeroným Zeidler.

The pseudo-Gothic architectonic pedestal with three salients bears standing figures of the three saints portrayed in the dry academic tradition which is typical of the work of both Maxes. On this site there originally stood a group of St. Norbert with St. Adrian and St. James, which, carved by Jan Brokoff, was built here in 1708 by the Strahov Abbot Vít Seipl.

In 1765 this group was pieced toge-

V. The staircase from the bridge to the island of Kampa. Builder Jos. Kranner. 1844.

again obviously covers the greater personality of his son, Ferdinand Max, whose authorship of the work is witnessed by its masterly composition and the high standard of its execution.

15. Statue of St. Ludmila. (Sandstone.) The date of origin is unknown, as are also the sculptor and patron. The statue was made for some other purpose (possibly for the castle ramparts) and was transferred to the bridge after 1784, when the group of St. Wenceslas fell into the water.

Judging by its style, an open grouping of the saint with her grandson, the little St. Wenceslas, and angels, standing on an architectonic pedestal decorated with a painted modelled relief of the murder of St. Wenceslas, it comes undoubtedly from the workshops of *Matyáš Braun* some time after 1720. The sensual conception of the Saint's face, the movement in the attitude and the illusion of fluttering draperies all bear the marks of Braun's art.

The group of St. Wenceslas, which stood here before, was built towards the ther and built anew, carved by the sculptor *Ignác Platzer* senior, and composed in the same way as its predecessor–only in place of the two saints there were statues of kneeling angels. A wooden model of Platzer's group is in the library of the Strahov Monastery in Prague IV.

16. Statue of St. John Nepomucký. (Bronze.)
Original from 1683. – Clay sketch for the statue: the Viennese sculptor *Mathias Rauchmüller*.
Wooden model: *Jan Brokoff, 1682.*
Bronze casting: Volfgang Jeroným Heroldt, Nurenburg 1683. Signature partly preserved.
Builder: Matěj, knight of Wunšvic.

This statue, showing the traditional conception of the saint as a bearded canon with a halo of stars, stands on a three-part pedestal in which there are three bronze cast tablets with scenes of the Confession of Queen Johanna, the Casting of the Saint into the Vltava and a votive inscription. Above this is a plastic bronze coat-of-arms of the donor of the statue, the knight of Wunšvic. Under the saint's right foot is the signature Heroldt and the date

---

VI. The lower Malá Strana Bridge Tower. Romanesque, from the second half of the 12th century. Renaissance details and plaster from 1491.

end of the 17th century at the expense of Václav Arnošt Markvart of Hrádek, imperial councillor and judge of the Kingdom of Bohemia. In the book of the bridge Octavian is named as the sculptor. Today the pedestal of the group stands on the ramparts of the Prague castle under Č. Vosmík's new statue, but the group itself is laid in the country lapidarium, and portrays an open group of three figures, St. Wenceslas in a semi-antique conception and two angels with his saintly attributes. It has all the characteristics of the free illusive style of the late baroque Roman sculpture, and judging from this fact, and also facts from other historical documents, we can assume that the Octavian who is named as the sculptor is the same as the sculptor *Octavio Mosto*, a native of Padua, who came to Prague in 1695 from Salzburg, and who is one of the first representatives of Roman sculptural baroque in Prague. Mosto died in Prague in 1701. Therefore this statue must have been built between this year and 1695.

1683, the year of the supposed three hundredth anniversary of the saint's martyrdom. The sketch of the statue is in the possession of the photographer Pešina in Prague XIX, and Brokoff's wooden model stands on the main altar of the church of St. John na Skalce (St. John on the Cliff) in Prague II. The cost of the statue amounted to 7000 guilders.

17. Group of St. Francis Seraphim (Sandstone.)

18. Statue of St. Anthony of Padua (Sandstone.)

VII. Votive relief on the facade of the lower Malá Strana bridge tower. Circa 1250. Opuka stone.

1855. – Sculptor: *Emanuel Max.*
Donor: František Kolovrat Lichsteinský.

On a pseudo-baroque pedestal stand three isolated figures of St. Francis and three angels in the academic classical style of the middle of the 19th century.

The group stands on the site of an older group, probably a composite one, which was built here in 1708 at the expense of Count Václav Vojtěch of Šternberg, the builder of the castle at Troja u Prahy and an outstanding patron of the arts. The sculptor of this group was the sculptor and innkeeper of Malá Strana, *František Preis.* (In J. J. Kamenitzký's work on the bridge sculptury of 1716 the author's mark is given as A. 1716 F. P.) The figures of this group, composed and modelled in the mobile baroque style were transferred before 1855 from the bridge in front of the facade of the Church of St. Josef in Prague II and separated. The statue of the saint is in the wall niche in front of the church court, and the two angels in the court itself.

Baroque original from 1707. – Sculptor: *Jan Oldřich Mayer.*
Builder: Krištof Mořic Withauer, Councillor of the Burgrave of Prague Castle.

On a simple prismatic pedestal stands the statue of the Franciscan saint, holding a voluted pedestal on which stands the infant Jesus. At either side of the statue there is a stone vase, the right one ornamented with a relief illustrating scenes from the legends of the saint.

19. Group of St. Vin cent of Ferrara and St. Prokop. (Sandstone.)

20. Statue of St. Juda Tadeas. (Sandstone.)

VIII. Malá Strana bridge towers and gate. The lower tower from the second half of the 12th century, the higher from 1464, and the gate from the second decade of the 15th century.

1712. – Sculptor: *Ferdinand Max Brokoff*.
Builder: Romedius Josef František
Count Thun, Lord of Choltice.

The high pedestal is ornamented
with three busts of a Turk, a Jew and
Satan as symbols of powers which were
either gained for the faith or humbled
through the personalities of the two
saints, and surmounted by a relief of
the Last Judgment, and a free conception of St. Prokop the ploughman. On
the left is the figure of St. Vincent in
Dominican garb, raising a man from the
dead. On the right is St. Prokop, in
Abbot's gown, standing on the devil.
On the back of the pedestal is Jan Brokoff's signature. However, looking at
the broad conception and style of modelling, it is evident here too that the
real author of the work is his son
Ferdinand. The reliefs on the pedestal
are in the older style of modelling, and
are probably the work of one of the
master's assistants.

In picturesqueness and magnificence
of presentation it is one of the most
remarkable groups on the bridge.

Under the group, on the capital of
the pillar of the bridge, stands a statue
of B r u n c v i k (sandstone). (Ill. 19b.)
1884. – Sculptor: *Ludvík Šimek*.
Builder: The City of Prague.

On a pseudo-Gothic prismatic panelled pedestal with symbolic figural decoration, stands the figure of a soldier
in armour of the 16th century. In his
right hand he holds an unsheathed
sword, and near his right foot is a shield
with the coat-of-arms of Prague Old
Town. Below the pedestal there are 11
shields with emblems the significance

Baroque original from 1708. – Sculptor:
Jan Oldřich Mayer.
Builder: František Sezima, knight of
Mitrovský of Nemyšl and Jetřichovice.

A current, rather static portrayal
of the saint with the usual attribute,
a cudgel, on a simple baroque pedestal
with a votive inscription.

of which is unknown, possibly they are the coats-of-arms of the townspeople who contributed towards the building of the original statue, carved at the beginning of the 16th century. In the course of time this statue decayed and eventually only the pedestal remained with the lower part of the statue. In the eighties the torso was laid in the country lapidarium and was replaced by the present work of Šimek's. The appearance of the statue can be seen from an alabaster copy from the first half of the 17th century which was exhibited in the exhibition "Acadia" in Prague in 1862, and which belonged to Knight Neuberg.

21. Statue of St. Michael Tolentine. (Sandstone.)

1708. – Sculptor: *Jan Bedřich Kohl.*
Builder: The Augustine Convent in Prague III.

A simple prismatic pedestal with voluted wings bears the statue of the saint, a friar, whose character as a benefactor of the poor is expressed by the figure of an angel with a basket of bread.

Behind this statue the balustrade of the bridge is broken by the entrance to the novo-Gothic two-flight stairway which joins the island of Kampa with the bridge. This was built in 1844 from a plan of architect *Josef Kranner's,* in place of the old bridge from 1785.

23. Statue of St. Luitgarda. (Sandstone.)

1710. – Sculptor: *Matyáš Bern. Braun.*
Builder: Evžen Tittl, Abbot of the Cis-

22. Statue of St. Augustine. (Sandstone.)

Baroque original from 1708. – Sculptor: *Jan Bedřich Kohl.*
Builder: The Augustine Convent of St. Thomas in Prague III.

The patron of the order and outstanding philosopher (†430) is portrayed in bishop's garb, in the wellknown tradition with an angel who is trying to pour away the sea with a shell. It has a simple architectonic pedestal with a votive inscription.

24. Statue of St. Gaetano, founder of the Order of Theatins. (Sandstone.)
Baroque original from 1709. – Sculptor: *Ferdinand Max Brokoff.*

tercian Monastery in Plasy. The cost was 1200 gilders.

This group, which is the most artistically valuable and most famous on the bridge, shows the Vision of St. Luitgarda the Cistercian sister from the Convent of St. Trond, when, as she prayed, she had a vision that Christ descended to her from the cross and let her kiss his wounds.

The group stands on an architectonic base, which, by its form appears to have been created by Braun's friend, the well-known Prague architect, František Max Kaňka. This statue shows in its purest form the faithful sculptural presentation, the composition of colours and naturalistic expression of the body and clothing, which are the marks of the height of baroque sculptural mastery, of power over their material, a style developed from the Roman sculpture of the 17th century, from the school of Lorenzo Bernini, of which Braun was the greatest and most exact disciple in Bohemia.

25. Statue of St. Adalbert. (Sandstone.)

1709. – Sculptor: *Josef Michal Brokoff?*
Builder: Markus Bern. Joanelli, a Councillor of the Old Town of Prague whose coat-of-arms is at the head of the balustrade, joined to the base with angels' bodies and akants. Below the statue of the saint, which is carried out in the native monumental but realistic style, is the signature of Jan Brokoff. But if we compare this statue with the other creative works of the old Brokoff, we can scarcely accept as the author of

Builder: Former convent of the Order of Theatins (Kajetáns) in Prague III. The cost was 774 gilders 45 crowns.

This statue is of noble conception, showing the saint († 1547) in the robes of his order standing on a corniced pedestal before an obelisk, covered with clouds and angels' heads and surmounted by a picture of a heart. The obelisk symbolises the Holy Trinity. At its foot is the signature of Jan Brokoff as the owner of the sculpture works from which the statue came. But according to the high artistic standard of the statue, it must be supposed to be an anonymous work of Jan Brokoff's collaborator, the young Ferdinand Max, whose artistry far surpassed that of his father. Similar cases of the signature being that of the owner of the workshop and not of the author of the statue, appear several times on the bridge and is quite a recognised thing in baroque sculptural practice.

26. Statue of St. Philip Benitius. (Saltzburg marble.)

Baroque original from 1714. – Sculptor: *Michal Bernard Mandl.*
Builder: Convent of the Order of Servites in Prague II.

This is the last work of the outstanding representative of Saltzburg baroque, and differs from the other sculptures on the bridge in being carved in marble. It portrays the general of the Order of Servites in an ecstatic pose, and stands on a simple prismatic pedestal (a copy from 1854) with a pseudo-

this deeply-felt figure the conservative wood-engraver Jan Brokoff. In form it is much nearer to the style of Brokoff's son Josef Michal.

27. Group of St. John of Matha, St. Felix of Valois and St. Evan. (Sandstone.)
1714. – Sculptor: *Ferdinand Max Brokoff.* Builder: František Josef Thun, a noble of Klášterec.

This is the most popular group of those on the bridge and also the most expensive and the largest, and was built in memory of the two founders of the Order of Trinitarians, founded when the Christians were rescued from the power of unbelievers. It is not known why the figure of the Slav patron St. Evan is coupled with the two French saints. The extremely picturesque and expressive conception of the group, which is typical of Ferdinand Brokoff's later work, shows the pedestal in the form of a cave, in which the three captive Christians are begging God for mercy. At the side of the cave window is a guard, shown as a Turk, and this is one of the most famous Prague statues.

Above the cave window is a triangular cartouche on which an angel, in relief, is seen freeing two captives, and also the coat-of-arms of the donor of the statue and his wife. This cartouche is held in one hand by St. Felix, while he gives his other hand to the freed christians. Above the Turk's head hangs the figure of St. John of Matha with a stag, whose apparition gave the impulse for the founding of the order.

rococo inscribed cartouche at the head. – The clay sketch for the statue is in the museum in Saltzburg, where the statue was carved.

28. Statue of St. Guy. (Sandstone). Baroque original from 1714. – Sculptor: *Ferdinand Max Brokoff.* Builder: Matěj Vojtěch Macht of Löwenmacht, deacon of Vyšehrad.

On an open architectonical pedestal in the form of cliffs and a cave, from which lions are crawling out (the symbols of the saint), stands St. Vitus in the current presentation of the Roman soldier with a princes' mediaeval cap on his head. In this portrayal the conception of the saint as a Roman noble, tortured for his faith, is linked with the story of the bones of his shoulders which were acquired as a remarkable cultural relic by the Czech priest of St. Wenceslas, and for which the third christian church was founded on the Prague castle hill. On the eastern side of the cliffs is the signature of Jan Brokoff, again only as the owner of the workshop.

A replica of this statue, also the work of F. M. Brokoff, is to be found in Radíčo near Sedlčany.

Above St. Felix is a kneeling figure of St. Evan with a typical Russian physiognomy.

Jan Brokoff's signature on the pedestal behind the Turk again only marks him as the owner of the sculptury works, and not as the author of the group.

29. Statue of St. Wenceslas. (Sandstone).
1858. – Sculptor: *Josef Kamil Böhm.*
Builder: The Klar's Institute for the Blind in Prague III. – The sketch for this statue was made by the painter Josef Führich. This fact and also the artistic sculptural design give a nazarene academic tension to the figure, standing calmly posed and empty of expression.

Until 1822 there was a row of small shops on the present site of this statue, running from the former toll house near the Malá Strana bridge tower to the group of St. John of Matha.

30. Group of Ss. Kosma and Damian. (Sandstone).
Baroque original from 1709. – Sculptor: *Jan Oldřich Mayer.*
Builder: The Medical Faculty of Charles University in Prague.

On a three-part architectonic pedestal, rather massive and disproportioned, there is a votive inscription with scrolls, and on this stand the three figures, quite unconnected with one another: the patrons of medicine with a statue of the Saviour in the middle. These are cut from the stone in the local Central European realistic style.

At the left end of the bridge going towards Malá Strana the former toll house, No. 56-III, encroaches onto the body of the bridge. This house was rebuilt into its present form in 1591, and the facade repaired in the middle of the 19th century. The date of this rebuilding is witnessed by the Latin inscription over the portal, which reads: Senatus antiquae urbis Pragensis aedificium veteris telonii ruinosum cum vicina turri refici curavit MDXCI. It can be seen from old illustrations that the house used to have a noble renaissance facade with interesting shields on it.

The inside of the house, which was originally the seat of the Old Town customs office and the imperial salt office, and also occupied partly by private tenants, contains many renaissance details, probably even today. The outside shows that it has been carefully preserved. In the upper storey there used to be many single corner rooms joined to the lower bridge tower by a pillared arcade, and entered from the arcade through a genuine contemporary portal with a trellised grill. The arcade is now for the greater part walled up and has been changed into living quarters.

It is not known when this house was built. It certainly was standing in 1544, when the bridge office, as it is literally recorded, let a room in the toll house to Thomas the gingerbread merchant for 40 gr. a year, for the purpose of his trade. This was obviously one of the small shops which enterprising merchants set up at the Malá Strana end of the bridge, and which the bridge office exploited for the upkeep of the bridge. In the 16th century there were altogether twelve of these shops, six on each side. After the battles in 1648 only five of them remained.

This building of the former toll house is built onto the lower Malá Strana bridge tower, one of the two towers which guard the entrance from the bridge to the smaller town of Prague. The present configuration is not the original one. The lower tower, of romanesque origin, is the remains of the fortification of the original Judith Bridge, and the opposite higher tower was built on the site of a former, undoubtedly also romanesque, tower in the 15th century. The date of the lower tower's being built can only be guessed approximately. It may have been built within the period of the building of the Malá Strana fortifications in the middle of the 13th century, but judging by the form of the square hewn stones in the walls, it is more probable that it was built at the same time as the Judith Bridge, in the second half of the 12th century. In 1591 it was repaired in renaissance style, and it is from this time that the ornamental shields and remains of rusticated rough-cast date, as well as the shape of the windows and the portal. Originally, until the completion of the toll house, this lower tower stood open towards the bridge, and in the period before the building of the present Charles Bridge it created an impression of greater height and slenderness, because the level of the Judith Bridge was lower than that of Charles Bridge. Certainly the eastern side of the tower was open in the middle of the 13th century, when on the first floor of the eastern tower wall an illustrative votive relief in opuka stone was erected. This relief, placed on the flat wall of a semicircular niche, was covered up at an unknown date, and rediscovered in 1888, when, however, owing to the lack of understanding of the tenants of the tower, it was again covered with a wooden panelling. In 1938, thanks to the care of the Club for the Preservation of Old Prague, the headquarters of which are in the tower, it was once more revealed and preserved. It shows a group of two people, both of life size. On the left, carved in profile, is a kneeling youth (the head, which is beardless, is today in the collection in the Prague City Museum) dressed in a tunic. On the right, facing the front, is the torso of a figure seated on a throne and dressed in a tight-fitting skirt and a coat, fastened on the right shoulder with a simple stone. The head, hands and feet of this figure are missing. The niche behind and at the sides of the relief were painted in polychrome with blue and black. For reasons of preservation, the relief is temporarily boarded up, until a grating has been made which should protect it from the touch of careless people. It is difficult to guess what this relief represents, though it is a remarkable memorial to

Czech sculpture of the period between romanesque and gothic. The most acceptable theory seems to be the recent one of C. Merhout's who explains that it is one of the memorials to Václav I, which were built in Prague after his death in 1254, and that the group portrays Přemysl II, kneeling humbly before his father Václav after his unsuccessful revolt.

The inside of the tower is divided into the groundfloor and three upper stories, and is entered through a portal from the passage of house No. 56-III, the former toll house. The floors are connected by a wooden staircase with an oak balustrade. There is a single, oblong room on each floor. From the highest one, where the staircase ends, there is a genuine entrance to the arch of the gate, and from there to the second higher tower, which has late renaissance oak doors ornamented with carving.

The gate between the two towers consists of two parallel Gothic pointed arcades, decorated round the circumference of the arches with crabs and raised flowers. The upper edge of the gate has battlements round it, and the surface of the gates are ornamented with coats-of-arms. On the surface facing the bridge these are, from left to right: the Luxemburg lion, the Czech lion and the Moravian eagle, and under them in the middle the emblem of Prague Old Town. On the other side, facing towards Malá Strana, there are between the battlements the coat-of-arms of Breslau (Vratislava), the Czech lion and the coat-of-arms of Lower Lusatia, and under them the emblems of the Old and Lesser Towns of Prague. According to these emblems of the wide extent of the power of the Czech king as it appeared in 1411, the bridge gate must have originated shortly after this year. There is a way, through this gate onto the bridge, from the lower tower to the higher tower.

The higher Malá Strana bridge tower is the youngest building of the bridge components. It was built in the second half of the 15th century and the foundations laid in 1464. It stands on the site of an older tower, of unknown form, but undoubtedly romanesque in origin, the existence of which is witnessed by indirect written records of the 14th century. The present higher Malá Strana tower is a remarkable building monument showing the artistic stagnation in the Prague gothic period after the Hussites. Its whole scheme and architectural decoration show the helplessness of this time, being a repetition of the project and basic outlines of Parler's decoration of the tower on the Old Town side. The prismatic cube of the tower is, on the main sides, decorated with canopied niches. These niches were obviously intended to contain statues of the builders of the bridge. Perhaps the plastic portrait of Jiří of Poděbrady, was to have stood here when the tower was finished, and possibly also the statues of his predecessors, thanks to whom the bridge was built, Charles IV and Václav IV. This supposition is supported by the fact that King Jiří had a great sence of plastic portraits. Perhaps this place was intended for the statue which is similar to that which he had immortalised on the shield of the church of the Virgin Mary at Týn, which was just finished during his reign. Why the niches in the bridge tower remained empty is not known. Perhaps the builders never had time to attend to their completion, or possibly they were destroyed in the later battles on the bridge. Whether it is for one reason or another, the mass of the tower is poor without the statue which should have stood here, and loses an architectural and plastic harmony.

V. INSCRIPTIONS ON THE TOWER
AND ON THE BRIDGE STATUES.

I. On the western side of the first floor of the Old Town Bridge Tower.

SISTE HIC PAVLISPER VIATOR SED LVBENS AC VOLENS
VBI MVLTA POPVLATVS TANDEM VEL INVITVS SISTERE
DEBVIT GOTHORVM ET VANDALORVM FVROR ET LEGE
SCVLPTVM IN MARMORE QVOD AD PERPETVAM BOHE-
MORVM OMNIVM SED IMPRIMIS VETERO PRAGENSIVM
MEMORIAM ANNO DOMINI MDCXLVIII MARS SVECICVS
FERRO ET IGNE IN HAC TVRRI DELINEAVIT. HAEC TVR-
RIS GOTHICI FVIT VLTIMA META FVRORIS SED FIDEI
NON EST HAEC VLTIMA META BOHEMICAE. VOLVISSENT
ID IPSVM CIVES VETERO PRAGENSES FVSO SANGVINE
INSCRIBERE NISI PAX AVREA FERDINANDI III. PIETATE
ET IVSTITIA IN ORBEM GERMANICVM REDVCTA PRO
SANGVINE AVRVM SVPPEDITASSET.
(Pilgrim, stand here gladly and willingly for a moment, where against
his will the devil of the Goths and Vandals was beaten. And read,
carved in marble, how in 1648 the Swedish army, to the eternal
memory of all Czechs and especially the citizens of the Old Town,
immortalised this tower by fire and the sword. This tower was
the last barrier of gothic fury, but not of Czech fidelity. The citizens of the Old Town would have shed their blood but for the
golden peace of Ferdinand III which, together with the revival of
religious belief and peance, changed blood by the gold of the letters.)

137

II. On the northern side of the ground floor of the Old Town Bridge Tower.

CAROLVS IV. AVG. PONTEM EXTRVXIT A. MCCCLVII.
VETVSTATE VITIATVM ET FLVMINIS GLACIEM DEVOL-
VENTIS IMPETV ANNO MDCCLXXXIV PENE DIRVTVM
IOSEPHVS II. AVG. INSTAVRARI, NOVISQ. SVBSTRVC-
TIONIBVS MVNIRI IVSSIT.
A. D. MDCCCLVII.
Haec tabula de pila pontis cui statua Sct. Christophori erat inpo-
nenda hunc in locum translata est.
A. D. 1857.
(The Emperor Charles IV built the bridge in 1357. It decayed with
age and was almost destroyed in 1784 by the concourse of waters
with floating ice. The Emperor Josef II commanded that it should
be repaired and new foundations laid.
This tablet was brought here from the pillar on which the statue
of St. Christopher should have stood.)

III. On the cornice of the portal of house No. 53-III, the former toll house.

SENATVS ANTIQ. VRBIS PRAG. ÆDIFICIVM VETERIS TELO-
NII RVINOSVM CVM VICINA TVRRI REFICI CVRAVIT
MDXCI.
(The Senate of the Old Town of Prague had the delapidated build-
ing of the old toll house and the neighbouring tower repaired in
1591.)

IV. On the statues and pedestals of the bridge statues.

1. The group of St. Ivon.
    Today this has no inscription.
    On the cartouche under the figure of the saint on the pede-
    stal, there used to be the following inscription:

(SANCTO IVONI IVSTITIAE SACERDOTI AC
PATRONO SVO FACVLTAS IVRIDICA IN VNI-
VERSITATE PRAGENSI PIE POSVIT ET SACRAVIT).
(To St. Ivon the priest of justice and his religious patron, this
statue was built and consecrated by the Faculty of Law of Prague
University: 1711.)

2. The Statue of St. Bernard.

On the scroll in the middle of the pedestal: AD GABRIELIS
AVE RESPONDES OPTIMA FIAT – REDDE TUUM FIAT
CUM REPETEMUS AVE – DAT BERNARDUS AVE, RE-
SPONDE OPTIMA SALVE – REDDE (TUUM) SALVE, CUM
REPETEMUS AVE.

(To Gabriel's Ave the most beautiful, you answer So Be It! - You
bring about your So Be it, if we repeat the Ave! - To Bernard's
Ave the most beautiful, you say Salve! - You bring about your
Salve if we again repeat the Ave! (This applies to the inscriptions which were on bands near the mouths of the two saints.)

On the scroll at the right: SI GABRIEL PROPRIUM VEL-
LET SIBI SUMERE VULTUM HANC BERNARDE TUAM
SUMERET EFFIGIEM. PRO GABRIELIS AVE RECIPIS
PATER OPTIME SALVE. PRO NOSTRO SALVE REDDE
PRECAMUR AVE.

(It Gabriel would consent to have his face removed, he would
take your image, Bernard. For Gabriel's Ave, you, greatest Father will receive Salve. For our Salve, grant us, we beg you, Ave.)

On the tablet at the right side of the pedestal: CHRISTO
MARIAE ET SANCTO PATRI BERNARDO POSVIT
A. D. MDCCIX. FRATER BENEDICTVS MONASTERII
OSSECENSIS ABBAS.

(The figures of Christ, Mary and St. Bernard were built by Brother Benedict, Abbot of the Monastery in Osek, A. D. 1709.)

3. The Group of Ss. Margaret, Barbara and Elizabeth.
   On the cartouche under the statue of St. Barbara (centre) ORATE PRO NOBIS NVNC ET IN HORA MORTIS. (Pray for us now and in the hour of death.)
   On the cornice under the saint's right foot: IOAN. BROKOFF FECIT. (Created by Jan Brokoff.)
4. The group of Ss. Thomas and Dominic.
   On the ribbon under the Madonna: IESV AC MARIAE DECORI.
   (Decoration of Jesus and Mary: 1708.)
   On St. Thomas's book: BENE SCRIPSISTI. (You have written well.)
   On the ribbon in St. Thomas's hand: AVE MARIA.
   On the scroll in the middle of the pedestal: MEMOR ESTO CONGREGATIONIS TVAE QVAM POSSEDISTI AB INITIO. (Be mindful of your congregation, which has belonged to you since the beginning.)
   On the cartouche at the right of the pedestal: SANCTO THOMAE AQVINATI DOCTORI. (To the Teacher of the Church, St. Thomas Aquinas: 1708.) POSITVS SVM EGO PREDICATOR ET DOCTOR IN FIDE ET VERITATE. (I became a preacher and teacher of faith and truth.)
   On the cartouche on the left of the right pedestal: SANCTO DOMINICO AVTHORI. (To St. Dominic the founder: 1708.) On the left side there was a similar, now illegible inscription: PREDICAMVS CHRISTVM CRVCIFIXVM IVDEIS QVIDEM SCANDALVM. (We believe in Christ the crucified, to the disgrace of all Jews.) On the pedestal's stylobat: PLANTABAT PREDICATORVM RELIGIO. (Founded by the order of priests 1708.)
5. The Group Piety.
   On the prominent flat pedestal: O vos omnes, qui transitis per viam, attendite et vidite si est dolor sicut dolor meus. (Oh all

ye who pass by, stop and see whether there is grief such as my grief.)

On the cliff under Christ: EM. MAX INV. ET FECIT 1859. (Conceived and built by Emanuel Max in Prague 1859.)

6. Group of the Holy Cross.

The Hebrew inscription in the arch over the cross means: Holy, Holy, Holy God.

On the shield under the eagle at the foot of the cross: RE-STAVRATVM A° MDCCVII. (Restored in 1707.)

On the shields on the cliffs is the Czech, Latin and German inscription: Thrice Holy, Holy, Holy. Founded to the greater glory of the crucified Christ, by the most illustrious royal tribunal of appelation, from a fine paid by a Jew who mocked at the holy cross, in the year of Our Lord 1696 on the fourteenth day of September.

On the border of the bridge balustrade: CAROLO ADAMO BARONI DE RZICZAN, QVI PERPETVVM HOC LVMEN ET SACRUM PERPETVVM METROPOLITANO SACELLO DIVI WENCESLAI FVNDAVIT, LEGATO BONO LAVNIO-WICZ SEDI ARCHIEPISCOPALI IOANNES FRIDERICVS ARCHI. EPISCOPVS PRAGENSIS HOC MONVMENTVM POSVIT A. MDCLXXXI. (To Karl Adam, Baron of Říčany, who endowed this holy light and eternal mass in the Metropolitan Chapel of St. Václav by his deed of the estate of Louňovice given to the archbishoprics, this memorial was erected by Jan Bedřich, Archbishop of Prague in 1681.)

7. Statue of St. Joseph.

On the plinth at the right: JOS. MAX inv. et fecit. (Invented and carved by Jos. Max.)

On the band on the tympany pedestal: Anno 1854.

On the main flat surface of the pedestal: Zum Andenken gewidmet von Josef Bergmann Bürger und Kaufmann in Prag. (In memory of Josef Bergmann, citizen and merchant of Prague.)

8. Statue of St. Anne.
No inscription.
9. Group of St. Francis Xaverius.
On the cartouche on the chased shield: SANCTO FRANCIS-
CO XAVERIO S. I. INDIARVM ET JAPONIAE APOSTOLO
THEOSOPHO GEMINAE FACVLTATES THEOLOGICA
ET PHILOSOPHICAVNIVERSITATIS PRAGis POSVERE
MDCCXI.
(To St. Francis Xaverius of the Society of Jesus, the apostle of
the Indians and Japanese, the beloved of God, erected by the
twin faculties of Theology and Philosophy of Prague University,
1711.)
10. Group of Ss. Cyril and Method.
On the pedestal: The signature of Karel Dvořák 1928 – 1938.
11. Statue of St. Christopher.
On the front of the pedestal: Ut Ille nos pelago saeculi jactatos
bracchio potenti perducat ad portum salutis quem mirum in-
fantem felix Christophore pie portasti per fluctus Te coeles-
tem periclitantium in undis Patronum cives precamur Pragenses. (Mayst thou guide us, who are tossed about in the sea
of ages, towards the harbour of salvation, as you carried the
marvellous child across the waves, this, oh celestial patron of
fearless sailors we, the citizens of Prague, beg of you.)
On the left of the pedestal: Cleri Pragensis duces et cultores
viribus unitis posuerunt. (Built by the Prague clergy and wor-
shippers together.)
On the right of the pedestal: Anno reparatae salutis
MDCCCLVII die festa S. Christophori. (In the year of salvation 1857 on St. Christopher's day.)
On the right side under the saint's foot: EM. MAX invenit et
fecit 1857. (Invented and carved by Em. Max 1857.)
12. Statue of St. John the Baptist.
Under the saint's left foot on the plinth: JOS. MAX INV. ET
FECIT. (Invented and carved by Jos. Max.)

13. Group of St. Francis Borgia.

Under the cordon of the cornice near the foot of the seated angel is the signature: IOANNES BROKOFF FECIT. (Created by Jan Brokoff.)

14. The group of St. Norbert.

In the middle of the pedestal: HONÓRI DIVI NORBERTI PA-TRIARCHAE SACRI AC CANONICI ORDINIS PRAEMON-STRATENSIS ATQUE PATRONI REGNI BOHEMIAE ANNO SALUTIS MDCCCLIII TERTIO IAM POSUIT VENERANDASQUE SS. REGUM VENCESLAI ET SIGIS-MUNDI IMAGINES ADIUNXIT LAETIS SUB AUSPICIIS VENERENDISSIMI AC MAGNIFICI HIERONYMI ZEIDLER PRAESULIS SIONEI CANONIA STRAHOVENSIS. (The statue of St. Norbert, patriach of the holy order of Canon Premonstrates, and patron of the kingdom of Bohemia, was erected in 1853 for the third time, and the statues of the patron saints Václav and Sigmund were added under the venerable patronage of the most dignified Abbot Jeroným Zeidler, by the canony of Strahov on the Sion.)

On the right of the pedestal: S. SIGISMVNDVS M. REX BVR-GVNDIAE PATRONVS BOHEMIAE REGNI CHRISTI PROPVGNATOR PERENNIS. (St. Sigmund, martyr, king of Burgundy, patron of the kingdom of Bohemia, eternal warrior for the kingdom of Christ.)

On the left of the pedestal: S. VENCESLAVS M. DVX ET PA-TRONVS BOHEMIAE DECVS SOLAMENQVE PATRIAE. (St. Václav, martyr, prince and patron of Bohemia, jewel and solace of his fatherland.)

On the plinth under St. Norbert's foot: IOS. MAX INV. et FECIT. (Projected and created by Jos. Max.)

15. The group of St. Ludmila.

No inscription.

16. Statue of St. John of Nepomuk.

In the middle of the pedestal: DIVO IOANNI NEPOMV-

CENO ANNO MCCCLXXXIII EX HOC PONTE DEIECTO EREXIT Mathias L. B. DE Wunschwitz ANNO MDCLXXXIII. (To St. Jan of Nepomuk, who in 1383 was thrown of this bridge, built in 1683 by Matěj, free baron of Wunšvic.) Under the saint's right foot: ME FECIT WOLFF HIERONI-MVS HEROLDT IN NVREMBERG 1683. (It was made by Wolff Jeroným Heroldt of Nuremberg in 1683.) Over the stone festoon on the right side of the pedestal is the inscription: BROKOFF FEC. (Made by Brokoff.)

17. Statue of St. Francis Seraphim.

On the middle part of the pedestal: SANCTO FRANCISCO SERAPHICO OB FRANCISCUM IOSEPHVM IMPERATO-REM AVGUSTVM MDCCCLIII DIVINITVS SERVATVM D. D. FRANCISCVS ANTONIVS COMES KOLOWRAT LIEBSTEINSKY EQVES AVREI VELLERIS MDCCCLV. (To St. Francis Seraphim, for the miraculous protection of the Emperor Francis Joseph in 1853, František Antonín Count Kolowrat Liebštejnský, Knight of the Golden Fleece 1855.) On the right of the pedestal: HE ORDERED HIS ANGELS TO GUARD YOU AND WATCH OVER ALL YOUR WAYS. PSALM 90. 11. (The same thing is written in German on the left face of the pedestal.) On the abacus under the statue of the saint: EM. MAX INV. ET FECIT. (Invented and created by Em. Max).

18. Statue of St. Anthony of Padua.

On the left of the pedestal: Deo InCarnato et sanC-to antonIo De paDVa erIgebat et DICabat C. M. V. (To God incarnate and St. Antony of Padua, erected and consecrated by C. M. V.: 1707.) The above inscription is today repeated on the right side. Originally there stood here the following: (ItaLIae proDI-GIose apostoLe regnI IosephI CaesarIs PROTEGE AMore.) (To the marvellous apostle of Italy,

defend with love the kingdom of the Emperor Joseph: 1708.)
On the head of the pedestal: : DEI GLORIAE ZELOTES
HOSTES IOSEPHI CAESARIS FERI TIMORE.(Oh you
zealots for the glory of God, strike fear into the enemies of
the Emperor Joseph: 1707.)

19. Group of St. Vincent of Ferrara and St. Prokop.
On the scroll over the coat-of-arms: S. S. VINCENTIO FER-
RERIO ET PROCOPIO BINIS PATRONIS D. D. D.
(To the two patron saints St. Vincent Ferrer and St. Prokop:
1712.)
On the coffin at the left: RESUSCITAVIT 40. (He raised 40
from the dead.)
On the pedestal cornice: CONVERTIT 100000 PECCATORES.
(He converted 100000 sinners.)
On the pillar of the left-hand carytid of the pedestal: 8.000
SARACENOS AD FIDEM CATHOLICAM. (8,000 heathen
to the catholic faith.)
On the pillar of the central carytid: 2.500 IUDAEOS AD
CHRISTUM. (2,500 Jews to Christ.)
On the pillar of the right-hand carytid: 70 DAEMONES DO-
MUIT. (He cast out 70 devils.)
On the back of the right of the pedestal: OPVS IOANNIS
BROKOFF. (The work of Jan Brokoff.)
On the tablet in relief on the pedestal: TIMETE DEUM ET
DATE ILLI HONOREM QVIA VENIT HORA IUDICII
EIUS. (Fear God and honour him, for the hour of judgment
is at hand.)

20. Statue of St. Juda Tadeas.
On the scroll of the pedestal: DEVOTO CHRISTI AMI-
CO. (To a devoted friend of Christ's: 1708.)

21. Statue of St. Michael Tolentine.
On the pedestal scroll (above): FIDELIVM CONSOLA-
TORI. (To the comforter of believers: 1708.)

On the tablet under the scroll: DIVO NICOLAO DE TO-
LENTINO PRODIGIOSA SANGVINIS EMANATIONE
PANEQVE BENEDICTO MIRACULA CONTINUA PAT-
RANTI (SACRVM.) To Saint Michael Tolentine, who perfor-
med miracles with miraculously emanating blood and sanctified
bread.)

22. Statue of St. Augustine.

On the pedestal scroll: DoCtorVM prInCIpI. (To the
prince of church teachers: 1708.)

On the pedestal tablet under the scroll: DoCtorVM prIn-
CIpI Magno Religionum Patriarchae Divo
Patri Augustino pietas filialis erexit. (To the
prince of church teachers, to the great patriarch of religion, to
the holy father of Augustine, this is erected in filial respect: 1708.)

23. Group of St. Luitgarda.

On the oval tablet on the pedestal: S. LUTGARDIS ORDINIS
CISTERCIENSIS. (St. Luitgarda of the Order of Cistercians.)
On the tablet on the right of the pedestal: VIVIFICUM
LATUS EXUGIT COR MUTUANS CORDE. EX BREV. CIST.
AD XV. IUNII. (The vivified side brought forth a heart, which
it exchanged for a heart. From the breviary of the Cistercians
for the 15th June.)

On the tablet on the left of the pedestal: CHRISTI CRUCI-
FIXI CONSTRICTA BRACHIO. (Through the constricted
arm of the crucified Christ.)

On the back of the pedestal: D. HONORI S. LUTGARDIS
POSUIT MONASTERIUM DE PLASS ORD. CISTERC. SVB
EVGENIO TYTTL ABBATE ET PRAEPOSITO S. M. MAGD.
AD BOH. LIPPAM MDCCX. (In honour of St. Luitgarda,
built by the Cistercian monastery in Plasy under the Abbot
Evžen Tyttl, Provost of St. Mary Magdalene's in Česká Lípa 1710.)

24. Statue of St. Gaetano.

On the book in the saint's hand: QVAERITE PRIMO REG-

NVM DEI ET IVSTITIAM EIVS ET HAEC OMNIA ADJI-
CIENTVR VOBIS. MATH. CAP. 6. V. 35. (Seek ye first the
kingdom of God and his righteousness, and all these things
shall be added unto you. Matt. chap. 6. v. 33.)

On the pedestal scroll: SANCTVS CAIETANVS THIENÆVS
CLERICORVM REGVLARVM FUNDATOR APOSTOLI-
CAE VIVENDI FORMAE IMITATOR. (St. Kajetán of Thien,
the founder of the Order, and the imitator of the lives of the
apostles.)

On the lower side of the pyramid at the right: IOAN. BRO-
KOFF FECIT ET INVENIT. (Invented and created by Jan
Brokoff.)

25. Statue of St. Adalbert.

At the bottom of the pedestal: MARCVS DE IOANELLI
REGIAE ANTIQVAEVRBIS PRAGENÆ CONSVLARIS
PVBLICO CVLTVI EXPOSVIT. (Marcus Joanelli, Coun-
cellor of the Old Town of Prague, built to show the public
his respect: 1709.)

26. Statue of St. Philip Benitius.

On the rococo scroll on the pedestal: PHILLIPPVS BENITIVS
ORDINIS SERVORVM B.V. M. Quintus Generalis in humili-
tate placvit DEO. (St. Philip Benitius, fifth general of the
Order of Servites, pleased God by his humility: 1713.)

27. Group of St. Felix of Valois, John of Matha and Evan.

On the right of the pedestal cornice: LIBERATA A CON-
TAGIONE PATRIA ET CONCLVSA CVM GALLIS
PACE. (When the country was freed from the plague, and
peace was concluded with the French: 1714.)

On the right-hand scroll: IOAN. FRANC. Ios. E. COMI-
TIBVS De THVN F. F. (Jan František Josef, Count of
Thun: 1714.)

On the pedestal, carved behind the Turk: OPVS IOAN. BROKOFF. (The work of Jan Brokoff.)

On the right side of the pedestal: Die Brückenstatuen wurden in Jahre 1854 durch Bürgermeister Dr. Wanka restauriert. (The bridge statues were restored in 1854 under the Lord Mayor Dr. Wanka.)

28. Statue of St. Guy.

On the abacus under the statue of the saint: S. VITVS.

On the cliffs at the right, over the lower lion: OPVS IOAN. BROKOFF. (The work of Jan Brokoff.)

29. Statue of St. Wenceslas.

On the main side of the pedestal: In memoriam festivitatis primae lustri quinti post fundationem instituti coecorum adultorum in Bohemia celebratae Pragae IV. in Octob. MDCCCLVII. (In memory of the first glorious quarter of a century since the foundation of the Institute for Blind Children in Prague, 4th October 1857.)

30. The group of Ss. Kosma and Damian.

On the cross: IN ISTA CRVCE NOSTRI REDEMPTIO. (In this cross is our redemption. 1709.)

On the cartouche under Christ: IESV CHRISTO ORBIS MEDICO. (Jesus Christ, the doctor of the world 1709.)

On the cartouche at the left of the pedestal: INTER DIVOS HIPPOCRATI COSMAE. (To Kosma, the Hippocrates of the saints: 1709.)

On the cartouche at the right of the pedestal: PIOQVE FRATRI COELI GALENO DAMIANO. (And to pious brother Damian, the Galen of heaven: 1709.)

On the vessels in the hands of Ss. Kosma and Damian: HIC MEDICINA VITAE. (This is the medicine of life: 1709.)

VI. LIST OF ILLUSTRATIONS.

A. THE STRUCTURE OF THE BRIDGE:

I. The Old Town Bridge Tower. *Peter Parler's* works. 2nd half 14th century.

II. Detail of the eastern side of the Old Town Bridge Tower. *Peter Parler's* works. Circa 1380.

III. Old Town Bridge Tower. Western side. 2nd half 14th century. First floor repaired 1649–50.

IV. Southern side of the bridge. In the foreground *Šimek's* statue of Bruncvik from 1884.

V. The staircase from the bridge to the island of Kampa. Builder *Jos. Kranner.* 1844.

VI. The lower Malá Strana Bridge Tower. Romanesque, from the second half of the 12th century. Renaissance details and plaster from 1491.

VII. Votive relief on the facade of the lower Malá Strana bridge tower. Circa 1250. Opuka stone.

VIII. Malá Strana bridge towers and gate. The lower tower from the second half of the 12th century, the higher from 1464, and the gate from the second decade of the 15th century.

B. SCULPTURAL ADORMENT:

1. *František Hergesel.* St. Ivo. A copy from 1908 of the original group of *Matyáš Bernard Braun* from 1711. Sandstone.

2. *Matěj Václav Jäkl.* The Madona with St. Bernard. 1709. Sandstone.

3. *Ferdinand Max Brokoff,* Ss. Barbara, Margaret and Elisabeth. 1707. Sandstone.

4. *Matěj Václav Jäkl.* The Madona with Ss. Dominic and Thomas Acquinas. 1708. Sandstone.
5. *Emanuel Max.* Piety (View with the cross) 1859. Sandstone.
6. Calvary. The bronze corpus of Christ from the period before 1657, pedestal from 1707, the statues of the Madonna and St. John Evangelist of *Emanuel Max.* 1861.
7. *Josef Max.* St. Joseph. 1854. Sandstone.
8. *Matěj Václav Jäkl*, St. Anne (Mother of the Virgin Mary). 1707. Sandstone.
9. *Čeněk Vosmík*, St. Francis Xaverius. A copy of 1911 of *F. M. Brokoff's* original group of 1711. Sandstone.
10. *Karel Dvořák*, St. Cyril and Method. 1938. Sandstone.
11. *Emanuel Max*, St. Christopher. 1857. Sandstone.
12. *Josef Max*, St. John the Baptist. 1855. Sandstone.
13. *Ferdinand Max Brokoff*, St. Francis Borgia. 1710. Sandstone.
13a. *Ferdinand Max Brokoff*, Angel. A detail of the group of St. Francis Borgia.
14. *Josef Max*, St. Norbert with Ss. Wenceslas and Sigismund. 1853. Sandstone.
15. *Matyáš Bernard Braun*, St. Ludmila and St. Wenceslas. Circa 1720. Sandstone.
15a. *Matyáš Bernard Braun*, St. Ludmila and St. Wenceslas. A detail.
16. *Mathias Rauchmüller*, St. Jan of Nepomuk. 1683. Bronze.
16a. *Mathias Rauchmüller*, The Queen's Confession. A detail of the pedestal of the statue of St. Jan of Nepomuk. Bronze.
17. *Emanuel Max*, St. Francis Seraphim with the angels. 1855. Sandstone.
18. *Jan Oldřich Mayer*, St. Anthony of Padua. 1707. Sandstone.
19. *Ferdinand Max Brokoff*, St. Vincent Ferrar and St. Prokop. 1712. Sandstone.
19a. *Ferdinand Max Brokoff*, A Jew. A detail from the group of St. Vincenc Ferrar and St. Prokop.
19b. *Ludvík Šimek*, Bruncvík. 1884. Sandstone.
20. *Jan Oldrich Mayer*, St. Juda Tadeas. 1708. Sandstone.
21. *Jan Bedřich Kohl*, St. Michael Tolentine. 1708. Sandstone.
22. *Jan Bedřich Kohl*, St. Augustine. 1708. Sandstone.
23. *Matyáš Bernard Braun*, St. Luitgarda. 1710. Sandstone.
23a. *Matyáš Bernard Braun*, St. Luitgarda. A detail.
24. *Ferdinand Max Brokoff*, St. Gaetano. 1709. Sandstone.
25. *Josef Michal Brokoff?* St. Adalbert. 1709. Sandstone.
25a. *Josef Michal Brokoff?* Cherub. A detail from the pedestal of St. Adalbert.
26. *Michal Bernard Mandl*, St. Philip Benitius. 1714. Marble.
27. *Ferdinand Max Brokoff*, St. John of Matha, St. Felix of Valois and St. Ivan. 1704. Sandstone.
27a. *Ferdinand Max Brokoff*, A Turk. A detail from the group of St. John of Matha.

27b. *Ferdinand Max Brokoff*, Imprisoned christians. A detail from
the group of St. John of Matha.
28. *Ferdinand Max Brokoff*, St. Guy.
1714. Sandstone.

29. *Josef Kamil Böhm*, St. Wenceslas.
1858. Sandstone.
30. *Jan Oldřich Mayer*, The Saviour
with Ss. Kosma and Damian.
1709. Sandstone.

C. OLD ILLUSTRATIONS OF THE BRIDGE AND ITS STATUES:

Supplement I. Charles Bridge in 1606. A detail of the prospect of Prague pu-
blished by J. Sadeler.
II. The Bridge about 1685. A detail of the prospect of Prague by
Folpert Ouden-Allen.
III. The Bridge about 1740. A copperplate of I. G. Ringle's from the
drawing by F. B. Werner.
IV. The Bridge in 1792. Part I. of the prospect of Prague by Joseph
Gregory from a drawing of L. Kohl's.
V. The Bridge in 1792. Part II. of the same prospect.
5a. *Jan Brokoff*, Piety. 1695. Copperplate of Neuräutter's from a drawing of
K. Kulík's from 1714.
7a. *Jan Brokoff*, St. Joseph. 1706. Copperplate of Neuräutter's from a drawing
of K. Kulík's from 1714.
10a. *Ferdinand Max Brokoff*, St. Ignace of Loyola. 1711. Copperplate of Neuräutter's from a drawing of K. Kulík's from 1714.
12a. *Jan Brokoff*, The Lord's Christening. 1706. Copperplate of Neuräutter's
from a drawing of K. Kulík's from 1714.
14a. *Jan Brokoff*, St. Norbert with the beatified Adrian and James. 1708.
Copperplate of Neuräutter's from a drawing of K. Kulík's from 1714.
14b. *Ignác Platzer*, St. Norbert with the angels. 1765. Copperplate of J. Salzer's
from a drawing of Ignác Platzers's.
15b. *Ottavio Mosto*, St. Wenceslas and the angels. End of the 17th century.
Copperplate of Augustine Neuräutter's from 1714.
17a. *František Preis*, St. Francis Seraphim and the angels. 1708. Copperplate of Neuräutter's from a drawing of K. Kulík's from 1714.

VIII. LIST OF ARTISTS.

Of Arass Mathias, architect 34

Of Avignon William, builder 41

Bendl Jan Jiří, sculptor 90, 96

Bernini Giov. Lor., sculptor 66, 73, 74, 130

Böhm Jos. Kamil, sculptor 86, 116, 132

De Bossi Campion Giovanni, architect 54, 57

Braun Matěj Bernard, sculptor 16, 64, 66, 68, 73, 74, 76, 82, 96, 98, 106, 118, 122, 129, 130

Brokoff Ferd. Maxm., sculptor 20, 38, 44, 52, 54, 58, 68, 70, 72, 73, 76, 78, 82, 84, 100, 108, 110, 114, 116, 120, 122, 128, 129, 180, 131

Brokoff Jan, sculptor 28, 34, 50, 60, 62, 68, 70, 72, 84, 108, 110, 114, 118, 120, 122, 130, 131, 132, 140, 143, 144, 145, 146, 147, 148

Brokoff Josef Michal, sculptor 102, 104, 130

Burgschmidt J., iron-moulder 92

de Corni Giulio, carpenter 56

Dvořák Karel, sculptor 42, 86, 114

Fischel Jeremiáš, wood-engraver 112

Fischer von Erlach Johann B., architect 80

Führich Josef, painter 132

Gregory Josef, painter 72, 88

Harovník Fabian, painter 112

Hähnel Ernst, sculptor 92

Hergessel Frant., sculptor 16, 106

Herget Frant. Leon., director of land buildings 57

Heroldt Wolf. Jeron., iron-moulder 122, 144

Jäkl Matěj Václav, sculptor 18, 22, 36, 74, 94, 106, 108, 114

Kaňka Frant. Maxm., architect 73, 130,

Klein's brothers, builders

Kohl Jan Bedř., sculptor 78, 92, 94, 129

Kranner Jos., architect, 57, 89, 120, 129

Kulík Karel, painter 28, 34, 44, 50, 60, 68, 78

Löw of Löwenberg, Mik., iron-moulder 112

Luragho Carlo, builder 18, 56, 92, 102

Maixner Petr, painter 98

Mandl Michal Bern., sculptor 80, 106, 130

Mathey Jean Bapt., architect 94

Max Emanuel, sculptor 26, 30, 46, 72, 74, 86, 110, 112, 116, 126, 141, 142, 145

Max Josef, sculptor 32, 48, 58, 72, 86, 114, 116, 120, 141, 142, 143

Mayer Jan Oldř., sculptor 78, 80, 90, 118, 126, 128, 132

Mocker Josef, architect 98

Mosto Ottavio, sculptor 64, 68, 74, 76, 82, 124

Neuräutter August., engraver 28, 34, 44, 50, 60, 64, 68, 78

Orsi Domenico, builder

Ouden-Allen Folpertus, engraver 40

Palliardi Ignác, architect 96

Parler Petr, architect 8, 10, 12, 34, 38, 40, 41, 42, 44, 98, 100, 102, 136

Platzer Ignác, sculptor 62, 82, 122

Prachner Richard, sculptor 94

Preiss Frant., sculptor 78, 126

Quitainer Filip Ondřej, sculptor 94

152

Rauchmüller Matyáš, sculptor 62, 68, 70, 74, 122

Reiner Václav Vavř., painter 94

Sadeler Jiljí, engraver 24, 62, 102

Salzer J., engraver 62

Soukup Jan, bridge engineer 58

Spinetti Giovanni, stonemason 56, 102

Süssner's brothers, sculptors 94

Šimek Ludvík, sculptor 14, 86, 128, 129

Traxal Frant., director of water buildings 57

Werner F. B., painter 56

Willmann Michal, painter 94

Vosmík Čeněk, sculptor 38, 114, 116

Wussin Kašpar, engraver 64

EPILOGUE.

When in 1943 the edition "Art Treasures" was renewed, its publisher offered me a re-publication of my book on Charles Bridge (Art Treasures, Volume 9, Prague, F. Topič, 1917) in an enlarged edition and with numerous illustrations. His offer was particularly attractive to me because I have a special affection for this work, which was my second book. I started to work on it as an official of the Museum of Prague, but I finished it only with the utmost exertion on one of the dirty straw mattresses of my war-time garrisons. I had prepared it very thoroughly without regard to its small size, and the material I had collected was so rich that I could not possibly use all of it. I had resolved therefore that I should return to the theme, especially as the new facts contained in my work had remained practically unnoticed, probably owing to the fact that no one expected to find anything new in a slender popular booklet.

I fulfilled my resolve only partially by editing the work on the first Prague stone bridge. There was so much material, and I then collected so much more, that from the two first introductory pages of this book there grew a scientific monograph "The Judith Bridge of Prague" (from 1920 – 1923, published in the Reports of the Memorial Department of the City of Prague, Volume 7, 1925, pp. 30–80, and further issued as a special publication in 1926). It was a monograph with a great wealth of annotations, a dull and – even to me – an unpleasant book, with which I wanted to prove that I could do a scientific work. However I did not continue in the same fashion in my work on the Charles Bridge.

I accepted the offer of the "Art Treasures", I soon saw, too lightheartedly. I was divided from the former two books not only by 25–30 years of life, but also by different circumstances, working conditions and interests which I had developed, so that my former scientific plans seemed to be a mere dream. Especially after the May revolution, it was impossible to find the time for a work which needed so much, considering that I should also have to study the new literature on the subject. Therefore I asked the editor of this edition to make the necessary revision as a co-author. Dr. Emanuel Poche willingly fulfilled this request, and he worked on the book with a rare understanding, leaving, where possible, my original text.

The basis of this book consists of my quoted works, which are connected, revised and enlarged with new scientific facts by Dr. E. Poche. So the book has now two authors, and – judging by the number of pages – I am not even the chief author. My collaborator has so enlarged the text, and added his own guide, explanations and documentation that, – thanks also to the splendid presentation – this is now another book, quite different from what was planned to be a mere new edition. I thank the co-author for his extensive and devoted work and also the publisher for the care which he has given to this publication.

Kamil Novotný.

I. The Prague Bridge in romanesque times 7
II. The Charles Bridge 32
III. The sculptures of Charles Bridge 60
IV. Guide to Charles Bridge 90
V. Inscriptions on the tower and on the bridge statues 137
VI. List of illustrations 149
VII. Index of artists 152
Epilogue 153

Authors: Kamil Novotný and Emanuel Poche
Title: Charles Bridge of Prague
Translator: Norah Robinson-Hronková
Published by: Pražské nakladatelství V. Poláčka,
                             (Prague publishing house V. Poláček)
                             Prague II, čp. 971
Year: 1947
Edition: Umělecké památky (Memorials of Art)
                             edited by Dr. Emanuel Poche
Arranged by: Petr Tučný
Blocks for illustrations: Jan Štenc
Supplements: Rotogravure Messrs. V. Neubert and Sons
                             and M. Schulz, Prague
Printed by: Státní tiskárna v Praze
                             (State printing house, Prague)
Edition: First 1–3000